Communal Angle in Indian Politics

Communal Angle in Indian Politics

Harish Sharma

Rawat Publications
Jaipur and New Delhi

ISBN 81-7033-637-6

The publication of this book was financially supported by ICSSR and the responsibility for the facts stated opinions expressed or conclusions reached, is entirely that of the author and that ICSSR accepts no responsibility for them.

ICSSR Consultant
Dr. Asghar Ali Engineer

Published by
Prem Rawat for ***Rawat Publications***
Satyam Apartments, Sector 3, Jain Temple Road,
Jawahar Nagar, Jaipur 302 004 India
Phone: 0141 651748 / 657006 Fax: 0141 651748
e-mail: rawatbooks@pinkline.net

Delhi Office
G-4, 4832/24, Ansari Road, Daryaganj, New Delhi 110 002
Phone: 3263290

Typeset by Rawat Computers, Jaipur
Printed at Nice Printing Press, New Delhi

Contents

Preface

This book is a revised version of the doctoral thesis that I had submitted to the university of Jamia Millia Islamia for the award of the Ph.D. degree in November 1996. The degree was awarded in 1997. A publication grant received from the Indian Council of Social science Research has facilitated this publication. It also gave me a second occasion to re-read the text and edit it with a view to updating.

The study focussed on the decade of the 1980s, and on the state of Uttar Pradesh. Therefore, even while revising that focus has not been changed although interesting developments have occurred since then in Indian politics that have a relevance to the theme of this study. Inclusion of new material would have extended the scope of the original study and further delayed the publication. I have, therefore, resisted the temptation for the moment in the hope that my future work will fill this gap.

The decade of 1980s has been a turning point in the history of Indian politics. After three decades of peaceful co-existence, suddenly communalism entered the centre stage. It shattered the fond hope of many that, with the passage of time, the country will forget the holocaust and the trauma of partition.

The process of development that ensued in the 1950s, and that changed the educational and economic profile of the country, was expected to erase the bruises of communal clashes and to usher in a culture of peace and communal harmony. The great Indian tradition of composite culture would, it was hoped, prevail and India will emerge as a good model of peaceful coexistence in the world.

But these hopes were frustrated by later day events. Despite the pronouncements by the founding fathers of the Indian Constitution, that the new State of India will be a secular polity, Indian political parties resorted to playing the regional, linguistic, religious and communal politics to garner political power. The arithmetic of vote motivated the political parties to invoke primordial loyalties in order to create their respective vote banks. Democratic politics, in the process, assumed the colour of communal politics.

Ever since 1952, when independent India first went to the polls, almost all the political parties attempted to mobilize people along caste and religious lines, but this was initially done covertly, almost in a clandestine manner, as no political party wanted to depart from the solemn pledge of building India as a secular democracy. But the politics of vote overwhelmed this pledge in subsequent elections when communal and regional considerations began to surface. The rulers of the princely states and the feudal chiefs who lost their special privileges, and the Hindu refugees who fled their homeland that became a part of Pakistan (and therefore nourished a special grudge against the Muslim community holding it responsible for its plight), became vociferous critics of "secularism". They viewed it as a garb to protect the interests of the Muslims at their cost. But these criticisms remained more at the verbal level, and the country did not witness any major violent clashes between the communities. The continuous victory of the Congress in elections, making it an unchallenged party in power, made the opposition parties impatient, almost desperate, to change the power equation. They took measures to strike the support base of the Congress, which was the minority communities, including the Muslims, and the oppressed groups within the Hindu society, called the "Scheduled Castes and Scheduled Tribes". Such reactions clearly got crystallized in the 1980s when the political parties came out openly, and started playing the communal card in the power game This brought the Bharatiya Janata Party (BJP) at the centre stage of Indian politics. Earlier, the political confrontation was between the Congress and the rest of the political parties. But, in the 1980s, BJP emerged as a major political force challenging the Congress.

While the BJP's emergence was seen, on the one hand, as an attempt to provide a viable national alternative in terms of challenging Congress hegemony, on the other, its aggressive and consistent stand on Ayodhya dispute came to be perceived by various religious and linguistic minorities, especially the Muslims, as a threat to their distinct identity and culture with the assertion of Hindu hegemony.

The Muslims are the second largest religious community in India, constituting nearly 12 per cent of the population. In a democratic polity, a minority community of this size cannot be ignored. The ruling Congress Party, as also other secular parties, cultivated this community for purposes of gaining its electoral support. The BJP---and its predecessor Bharatiya Jana Sangh---followed the other path of consolidating the non-Muslim votes by exploiting the religious sentiments of the majority community on issues such as Ayodhya dispute, Article 370, and the demand for Uniform Civil Code. It also challenged the secular policy of the Congress by calling it "pseudo-secular". A new debate was launched by BJP in the country on the concept of secularism.

It is this changing context that has prompted the present researcher to investigate the phenomenon of rising communalism in the country particularly in the 1980s. Obviously, it would have been a titanic task to cover all the facets of this controversy and to examine its various manifestations in the country of such a large size. It was, therefore, decided to focus on one single state and see how communalism was growing there. The choice of Uttar Pradesh appeared to be the obvious one. This is the State that has a large Muslim population not only in numbers but also in percentage terms---a higher average than the country as a whole. In the 1980s, it also became a focus of attention for the whole country because of the country-wide agitation in regard to the construction of a temple of the Hindu God Ram at the site where stood a sixteenth century mosque constructed by the Mughal Emperor Babar---known as Babri Masjid. While the legal dispute about the ownership of this plot of land had a long history, it suddenly assumed India-wide concern when the contending Hindus made it an issue of faith and even alleged that the mosque was built after the Muslims had destroyed the temple, and also claiming that the site was sacred to them as being the birthplace of Lord Ram. This was a claim that cannot be documented; it belonged to the realm of belief.

The study of communalism in the State of Uttar Pradesh, it was hoped, would provide insights for understanding the political dynamics. The decision was also taken to restrict the scope of the study by focusing only on the events of the 1980s when the Ayodhya controversy became so very prominent.

This study is, thus, a modest attempt to understand, in the broader context of communal and secular politics of India, the mobilization strategy of BJP through which it was able to increase its popular support base in the general elections of the Lok Sabha and Vidhan Sabha in Uttar Pradesh.

Covering a period of a decade, this study had to take recourse to secondary data rather than empirical field survey. I made use of the newspaper and magazine files, other published documents and books, and statistical tables generated by the Centre for the Study of Developing Societies (CSDS) to analyse election results. Besides, I informally interviewed a number of knowledgeables to check the facts and to ascertain the views and opinions from among both the Hindu and the Muslim leaders.

In carrying out this study, I have received help from several quarters. First of all, I will like to acknowledge my debt to Professor Z. A. Nizami, of the Department of Political Science at the Jamia Millia Islamia, who supervised the study. Without his valuable guidance and unflinching support, it would have been difficult to complete this assignment within the stipulated time.

The earlier drafts of my thesis were reviewed by Professor M. N. Meenai and Professor Z. M. Khan of the Department of Political Science at the Jamia Millia, and Dr Partha Ghosh of the Indian Council of Social Science Research. I am thankful to all of them for their helpful comments and observations.

I must thank Mr Yogendra Yadav of the Centre for the Study of Developing Societies (CSDS), who was kind enough to spare his time to discuss with me my material and offer valuable advice.

My friend, Dr Sunil Kumar Chaudhary, Lecturer in Political Science at the Shyam Lal College of the Delhi University, took pains to carefully go through the manuscript to check any errors that might have inadvertently crept in. As a friend and colleague I indeed treasure his moral support and academic help.

It will only be a formality if I were to thank my elder brother, Professor Yogesh Atal who was then Principal Director of Social and Human Sciences at UNESCO, Paris. While not faltering in his affections towards me, he never failed to impress upon me the importance of being academically vigorous, and hard working. Now that he has returned to India upon retirement, I could get his help in revising the study and preparing the press copy. His wife, Seema Atal's constant interest in my work deserves a special mention.

I received continuous encouragement from another brother, Dr Muktesh Sharma and from my dear sisters, Durga, Geetika and Meenakshi, as also from my childhood friend, Satyendra Javeria. The blessings of my in-laws—Professor D.D. Sharma and Mrs Suman Sharma---were a constant source of inspiration. They keenly followed the progress of my work and eagerly awaited the day when the degree was to be conferred.

My wife, Jaishree, courageously accepted to take over many responsibilities of the household to spare me the time to attend to my work. My children—Sangya and Sankalp—also cheerfully suffered my neglect; in fact, seeing me work also indirectly encouraged them to emulate me and concentrate on their studies.

Above all, I am reminded of my dear father, Shri Daulat Ram Sharma, who very much wanted me to do my Ph. D. Alas, he is not here to see his dream come true; but this piece of research is, indeed, a tribute to his memory.

I will be remiss in my duty if I were not to thank the helpful staff of the libraries of the Indian Council of Social Science Research, Indian Council of Historical Research, Indian Institute of Public Administration, and the Nehru Memorial Museum and Library---these were my frequent haunting places for all these years I was working on this project.

Harish Sharma

1

Introduction

The seeds of communal disharmony sown by the British during the colonial period, as part of their policy of "divide and rule", changed the political landscape of India. While the British failed to retain their hold over the Indian territory and had to finally quit the country, they succeeded in partitioning the subcontinent into two dissimilar nations and creating a feeling of mutual distrust and animosity among the Hindus and the Muslims---the two major communities that populate independent India. The huge refugee influx from the region that now constitutes part of Pakistan added more colour to communalism. These Hindu refugees carried the scars of partition deeply embedded into their memories. The loss of their land and property, the shock of witnessing brutal murders of their kith and kin by the fanatic usurpers, cruel rapes of their women, and desecration of their places of worship were happenings that haunted them and provoked among some of them hatred and a feeling of revenge.

The trauma of India's partition in 1947, that accompanied its independence from the British rule, further fostered the ambivalent relationship between the Hindus and the Muslims.

During the last five decades, the country witnessed several situations of conflict and violence, involving the two communities. Communalism has become more aggressive and manifests itself not only in violent clashes but also in several fissiparous tendencies. State after state is being hit by organised communal violence not only in the urban metropolitan centres but also in rural areas. Political parties mobilise their support on communal lines; not only are there communal parties, even the so-called secular parties act communally. Such developments threaten the solidarity of the country and weaken national integration. Rise of communal tendencies is, thus, a cause of constant worry.

Unlike Pakistan, the post-independent India continued to be a plural society. To quote Atal, "What remained of India after the tragic episode of 1947 could not be described in religious terms---the original India was not divided between a Muslim Pakistan and a Hindu Bharat. The residual was several times larger than the seceder, and was pluri-cultural and pluri-religious. The decision that the state will have no religion, unlike Pakistan, led to calling the Indian polity *secular*."[1] The country is composed of several religious communities and ethnic groups including a significant Muslim population of more than 115 million. Obviously, no state with such a plural society could be formed on the basis of religion. However, it was not only a compulsion but also a commitment of the founding fathers of the Indian Constitution who converted India into a:

> *Sovereign, Socialist, Secular, Democratic Republic, to secure to all its citizens: Justice, social, economic and political; Liberty of thought, expression, belief, faith and worship; Equality of status and of*

1. Yogesh Atal, "Ideological Proximities, Political Distances", *Young India*, April 24 and May 1, 1999, p.4.

opportunity; and to promote among all Fraternity, assuring the dignity of the individual and the unity and integrity of nation.[2]

The secular constitution of India continues to serve as the guidepost for her polity. The constitution is, however, only a normative principle, a formula. The way it is translated into practice and the manner in which the people use the framework, provide the profile of an actually existing reality that is invariably a departure from the "ideal". Recent trends indicate that secularism, as an instrument of communal harmony, seems to have failed in achieving its goal. Notwithstanding the secular zeal of India's founding fathers, political compulsions and prevailing circumstances in post-independence India have eroded the secular ethos. In fact, the concept of secularism, as an antidote to communalism, has been greatly distorted by the various political parties in pursuance of their particular political goals. The original meaning of secularism as a device for achieving communal harmony is nearly lost. There is in evidence a continued accentuation of religious conflicts.

In this regard, it is important to note that the decade of the 1980s witnessed rise of religious fundamentalism in a number of Islamic states. This phenomenon also affected India. Political parties formed on communal basis took advantage of the situation and intensified their efforts to enlarge their membership and canvas for a political mandate. This happened on both the sides, and not just in the case of Muslims. For example, Bharatiya Jan Sangh, and its successor the Bharatiya Janata Party, gained popularity over the years as is evident from its performance at the polls. From just two seats in the Lok Sabha in 1984 it succeeded in winning 119 seats in 1991. Its strength in the 11th Lok Sabha(1996) increased to 161; and in

2. Preamble to the Indian Constitution.

the 12th (1998) and the 13th (1999) Lok Sabha it maintained a clear lead of 182 seats emerging as the single largest party breaking the monopoly of the Congress. Way back in 1967 elections, it recorded remarkable success in Vidhan Sabha elections throughout northern India and routed the Congress party. The party took the reins of the states of Himachal Pradesh, Madhya Pradesh, Rajasthan, and Uttar Pradesh in 1991. Even today, it continues to rule Gujarat and Himachal Pradesh, and is a leading coalition partner in the states of Haryana, Orissa and Uttar Pradesh. As a result, communalism in the present context is seen in terms of the rise of the Bharatiya Janata Party (BJP), the growth of other communal parties and pressure groups, and the continuation of communal violence, as well as alleged attacks on minority communities—the Muslims, Christians, and the Dalits and Scheduled Tribes. The trend is toward politicisation of the communal factor.

Different parts of the country have variously contributed to this emerging political culture of communalism. Apart from religious riots and protests at local community levels, there have been attempts to organise mass movements on communal lines. In addition to the Rashtriya Swayamsevak Sangh (RSS) and the Muslim League, there have been several other parties or movements that have contributed to communal strifes and tensions. The Shiv Sena movement in Maharashtra, the demand for Khalistan in Punjab, and the Muslim demand for secession in Kashmir are examples of the growing trends of communalism in Indian polity.

Communal tensions were fuelled by the much-debated Shah Bano case and the controversy surrounding Ramjanmabhoomi-Babri Masjid. It was on these religious issues that the two communities mobilised support from all over India and attracted worldwide attention. The 1989 parliamentary elections virtually came to be dominated by the aforementioned issues which adversely affected the Congress resulting in the loss of power at the Centre; even the subsequent government of V.P. Singh fell owing to the then prevailing communal controversies. The Babri Masjid issue brought to the fore the role of communalism and put at stake the secularist claim of the Indian State. Communalism has, thus, emerged as a major obstacle to the building of a modern, secular and democratic society. Although communalism has always been there in Indian society, the use of it for political bargain is a new phenomenon.

What are the deep-rooted factors that have kept communalism alive as a potent force in our society even after the partition of the country? What is the relationship of democracy with communal tensions? Morris Jones is of the view that "a relationship between democracy and separatism is at best ambiguous. On the one hand, democracy with its emphasis on accommodation and mutual bargaining encourages an attitude, which can accommodate genuine demands. At the same time, the type of competitive politics that invariably gets associated with democracy also gives rise to a situation of exaggerated demands, which, in turn, feed conflict, give rise to counter demands and become more and more difficult."[3]

Communalism became an integral part of Indian politics ever since the British rulers introduced the principle of elected representation in public institutions. Religious and communal identities have been exploited for electoral purposes. In the early years, it were the minority communities who complained of discrimination and highlighted their deprivations for political gain. In the later years, it is the majority community of the Hindus that has also been mobilised on religious and communal grounds to confront the Muslim community. BJP's

3. W.H. Morris Jones, *The Government and Politics in India*, Hutchinson, London, 1971, p. 19.

campaign for the construction of the Ram Temple at Ayodhya at the site of the Babri Masjid is the latest example of such an effort.

The decade of the 1980s has been a period of intense communal problems in India. This decade is considered as the most violent decade of the century when a total of 4,003 riots took place that is nearly the double of the previous decade when a total number of 2,574 riots took place.

In the 1980s there were several communal issues that created conflicts and posed threats to the unity of India. These were: Meenakshipuram conversions of Dalits to Islam; the demand for Khalistan by Sikhs in Punjab leading to Operation Blue Star; Assam agitation; demand by Kashmiri Muslims for secession; a series of intense communal riots in Moradabad, Allahabad, Meerut, Ahmedabad, Hyderabad, Bombay-Bhivandi, Aligarh, Muzaffarnagar, Bijnor; and mobilisation of Hindus for construction of the Ram Temple by the Vishwa Hindu Parishad (VHP) at the site of Babri Masjid, resulting in major Hindu-Muslim clashes not only in Ayodhya but throughout the country in 1992.

This decade also witnessed dramatic change in the policies of the Congress party. After suffering defeats in its strongholds in Karnataka and Andhra Pradesh and facing strong resentment by aggressive minorities in the border states of Jammu & Kashmir, Assam, and Punjab, the Congress party realised that it could no longer depend only on the voting support of the minorities. Therefore, it evolved a new strategy. This strategy, to quote Rajni Kothari, "had built into it the promise of winning back some of the earlier social bases too. It is quite interesting that immediately after the army action in Punjab, Mrs. Gandhi was in Garhwal and said openly and directly that the Hindu *dharma* was under attack. And, she made an impassioned appeal to save the Hindu *sanskriti* from the attack that was coming from the Sikhs, the Muslims and others. (T)he point is that even one such speech gives away the more blatant, much less massed, communal lines that the ruling party was adopting in 1984. From Operation Blue Star to the ouster of Abdullah to the post-assassination carnage to the election campaign of Rajiv Gandhi, *this* part of the strategy was perfected. And it indeed brought back a lot of lost ground."[4] The Congress party, thus, adopted a rightward shift, alongside the communal appeal, highlighting the "threats to India's unity by aggressive minorities". This paid dividends in the elections of Jammu & Kashmir Legislative Assembly and the Delhi Municipal Corporation. The Congress party also entered into an alliance with Shiv Sena in Maharashtra in municipal elections.

The right wing party of the country---the BJP, which suffered humiliating defeat in the 1980 elections of parliament[5]---realising that its main poll plank that "Hinduism is in danger" was being used by the Congress party, took immediate steps to protect its carefully carved out Hindu vote bank. In this connection, it found it politically profitable to support VHP's movement for the construction of Ram Temple at Ayodhya at the site of the Babri Masjid. In order to get power, both parties---the Congress and the BJP---started arousing religious sentiments of Hindus and Muslims. It was for the first time after the partition of the country that the two communities came in such direct confrontation, threatening once again the unity and secular identity of India. The political mobilisation of both communities over the Ayodhya dispute polarised the Indian society into two religious camps---the Hindus and the Muslims. The country witnessed a series of

4. Rajni Kothari, *State Against Democracy: In Search of Humane Governance*, Ajanta Publications, New Delhi, 1988, pp.247-8.
5. In this election the BJS was a coalition partner of the Janata Party. This combine got only 31seats, coming down from a previous total of 295 seats (1977 elections).

communal riots and destruction of property not only in Ayodhya but at large number of places.

This incident helped BJP in enlisting support of the majority community; its membership increased dramatically. It was able to increase its parliamentary seats from two in 1984 to 85 in 1989, 119 in 1991 and 161 in 1996 elections. Earlier, the National Front government of V.P. Singh fell only because of this issue. The heavy losses suffered by the Congress in 1996 elections can also partly be attributed to its failure to protect the Babri Masjid, which was demolished on 6 December 1992 by Hindu fanatics; it is alleged that Congress lost its Muslim vote on account of that failure.

Since communalism turned violent in this decade worries were expressed in certain quarters about the fate of Indian democracy. Some scholars thought that the growth of communalism is a dangerous trend and if it were allowed to grow it would change the very nature of Indian polity. There were others who regard this development as an indicator of the functioning of our democracy for, democracy allows its citizens to articulate their various demands and make it incumbent on the government to respond to them within the framework of the constitution.

The rise of unprecedented communalism provides a challenging and important opportunity for empirical investigation. Since Uttar Pradesh was a centre stage for this intense communal mobilisation by various political actors, this researcher decided to choose this state for study. The purpose of the present study is to document the process of politicisation of the masses on communal lines. It traces the growth of communal trends in Indian politics since independence and against this background it attempts to reconstruct the case of Ramjanmabhoomi-Babri Masjid. While analysing the mass upsurge among the Hindus over this issue and the Muslim response to it, the study examines the genesis of this issue, the role of its mobilising agents—Bharatiya Janata Party, Rashtriya Swayamsevak Sangh, Vishwa Hindu Parishad—and its effects on the Lok Sabha and Vidhan Sabha elections. For reasons of logistics, the study has concentrated only on the decade of the 1980. However, later-day developments have been indicated, where considered relevant.

The following chapter outlines the conceptual framework. It tries to analyse various definitions of communalism offered by several scholars to work out a definition based on that analysis.

The third chapter deals with the growth of communalism in India tracing its history and the consequences, ultimately culminating in the partition of the country. The post-partition communal scenario with a focus on the present-day communal politics has also been attempted in this chapter along with the analysis of major factors encouraging the growth of communal environment in the country.

The fourth chapter seeks to examine the growing phenomenon of communalism in the state of Uttar Pradesh during the 1980s. It discusses this problem in the state of pre-independence India, the role played by the Muslim League in the state, present demographic profile of the population, the major communal riots in post-independence India, the analysis of riots of the 1980s, implications of the judgment in Shah Bano case and communal mobilisation of the masses on the Ayodhya dispute as well as its repercussions.

In the fifth chapter a study of the genesis of the Ramjanmabhoomi-Babri Masjid controversy with legal and historical aspects has been attempted. The role of different political parties in dealing with this controversy as well as the role of vernacular press of Uttar Pradesh has been discussed.

In the sixth chapter the role of communalism in the parliamentary and assembly elections of Uttar Pradesh during the 1980s has been examined. An attempt has also been made to analyse the impact of the Ayodhya dispute on the performance of the political parties in Lok Sabha and Vidhan Sabha elections. In particular, an analysis has been made of the Muslim vote and Muslim politicians in terms of their number in both Lok Sabha and in the Vidhan Sabha, the size of the Muslim electorate, and the party affiliations of the Muslims in Uttar Pradesh. In doing all this, care has been taken to assess, to the extent possible, the impact of Ayodhya dispute on the performance of different political parties.

The concluding chapter attempts to focus on the issue of secularism, challenges to the secular identity of the country posed by the Ayodhya dispute and the role of the political parties in streamlining the communal politics in the country.

2

Communalism: A Conceptual Analysis

Communalism is an extremely complex phenomenon. It is generally associated with plural societies. While in the West communalism alludes to the feeling and a concern for the community, in India, the term has a negative connotation; it is used to designate the process of mobilising a community to confront another community. More specifically communalism is regarded as a manifestation of confrontation between the minority community and the majority community. In such situations, the over-concern with one's community is reflected in an antagonistic feeling towards other communities. When members of a community are negatively oriented towards other communities within their own society, they are supposed to inflame community feelings.

It is the negative connotation of the word 'communalism' that has received the widest currency in India. Understood as hatred and ill-feeling towards other communities, communalism seriously challenges the integrity of the nation, disturbs the peace of the country, and becomes a barrier to national integration. There exists a good deal of literature on communalism in India, but most of it is politically charged, and is journalistic in character. It is obvious that everything that happens in Indian society which is disruptive, and which threatens national integration, cannot be attributed to communalism. But, it is a convenient scapegoat. People easily buy an explanation of a public disturbance when it is couched in communal terms.

Speaking positively, communalism simply implies a concern for the community, a feeling of belonging to one's primordial group. It could as well be another name for "in-group solidarity". Students of group dynamics are familiar with the phenomenon through which people distinguish a member from a non-member in reference group terms. One qualifies to be a member of a group: (i) when the person explicitly owes his/her allegiance to a group, (ii) when "others belonging to that group" accept his/her claim, and (iii) when "others not belonging to that group" recognise that person as belonging to that group in question. Groups, thus, exist so long as there is such an allegiance and when both the members and the non-members recognise them. Such membership decides a person's both in-group and out-group orientation.[1] In modern society, a person belongs to several groups and, thus, his/her loyalties to any particular group remain divided and limited. But certain groups claim more loyalty than others. Groups based on the "ascribed status" belong to this category as the status of membership comes with one's birth. The groups in which a person enters due to his/her "achieved statuses" are of a different type. People can enter such groups at will and may decide to quit on their own; similarly, the group itself performs the gate-keeping function by restricting entry only to the

1. Yogesh Atal, *Dynamics of Nation Building: Communities in Crisis Situations*, Vol.II, UNESCO/RUSHSAP, Bangkok, 1988, pp. 8-9. For Reference Group Theory, see Robert Merton, *Social Theory and Social Structure*, The Free Press of Glencoe, London, 1957, Chapters VIII and IX.

qualified and ostracising those who disqualify or fall short of expectations. Usually, such groups do not demand too much loyalty from their members.

There is also an intermediate category of "ascribed status" groups in which people are admitted through "achievement". New religious groups belong to that category which allows new membership not only through ascription but also through achievement, that is, through conversion---a process of proselytisation. The newer the religion, the greater is induction of membership through conversion; over a period of time, it begins to have its members through birth, putting restrictions on recruitment through conversion. Reference Group Theory suggests that people who enter such groups demonstrate a renegade behaviour and show excessive zeal than the original members.[2]

In societies that are homogeneous in terms of language, culture, and religion, the word 'communal' is used as a positive term, as an expression of group solidarity, a "concern for the community". Community, in such cases, is defined in terms of space occupied by it—a village, a town, a habitat, or even a complete tribe residing at a given location.

But communalism assumes a different meaning in societies that are pluralistic, such as India. Described as a melting pot of races and a mosaic of religions and cultures, India has a history of several aggressive migrations. After initial confrontation between the aggressors and the local inhabitants there always ensued a subsequent process of accommodation and assimilation. In the process, there has been considerable interchange of various cultural traits and patterns, and racial and religious miscegenation. Many locals also got converted to arriving religions.

India is a multi-religious country. At the moment, the

2. See Merton, *Ibid.*

country has adherents of six major world religions which are spread all over the country and which could be found in all the eighteen major linguistic groups. Below is given the distribution of population in these religious groups in the censuses of 1981 and 1991.

Table 1

Population of India by Religion in 1981 and 1991

Religion	*1981*	*1991*	*% 1991*
Buddhist	4,719,900	6,387,500	0.76
Christian	16,174,498	19,640,284	2.34
Hindu	549,724,717	687,646,721	82.00
Jain	3,192,572	3,352,706	0.40
Muslim	75,571,514	101,596,057	12.12
Sikh	13,078,146	16,259,744	1.94
Other	2,826,502	11,419,676	0.39
Total	665,287,849	846,302,688	100.00

It is interesting to observe that while the census makes separate enumerations of the Jains, Sikhs and Buddhists, these are all clubbed together as Hindus when the media report any confrontation with the Muslims. Similarly, the fact that the Muslims are also divided into different sects such as Shia, Sunni, and Ahmedia is ignored. It was only recent that the Sikhs began asserting their separate identity to distinguish themselves from the Hindus in order to make a claim for a separate state of Khalistan. The Buddhist group also came into prominence after the mass conversion of people from the so-called "scheduled castes" under the influence of Ambedkar.

Communalism, in the Indian context, thus, has mainly been used to describe the tensions between the Hindus and the Muslims, the former being the majority, and the latter a minority. It is important to mention that the Muslim population in India is significantly large in real numbers although it constitutes around 12 per cent; the population of Muslims in India is third in the world, after Indonesia and Bangladesh. India has more Muslims than the population of Pakistan. Despite such a large size, it is viewed as a minority vis-à-vis the Hindus in percentage terms.

The British policy of "divide and rule" led to the formation of communal identities. The rulers allowed "language and ethnicity insulations to grow so as to keep the people divided. The epigenetic seat of central power had a wider knowledge base that covered all the sub-systems or the peripheries. While the peripheries were kept at a distance from each other, as if they were complete systems by themselves sharing little with others and constantly afraid of 'others' lest they should devour their identity and deprive them of their minority/ethnic privileges."[3]

Introduction of electoral politics as part of the process of democratisation further cemented the process and helped in making communal sentiments into a sort of "ism"—an ideology.

It is for this reason that some scholars consider communalism as an outgrowth of religious and cultural differences between the Hindus and the Muslims. These differences have created antagonism and distrust between them. Thus Rafiq Khan regards communalism "as a form of indifference, condescension, hatred, an aggressive attitude towards all the members of the religious community than one's own based on a real or imaginary threat from an individual or a group of that community.[4] In the same vein, Ratna Naidu says that a "communal situation is characterised by tensions between culturally distinct but geographically intermingled

3. Yogesh Atal, *op. cit.*, pp. 8-9.

4. M. Rafiq Khan, *Forms of Communalism, National Integration, Its Meaning and Relevance*, Navchetna Prakashan, Varanasi, 1970, p. 201.

communities".[5] Her qualification of the "geographical base" is very significant as that provides the arena for interaction.

Most authors agree that communalism as an ideology prevails only when two or more communities become "negatively oriented" to each other. It is in this sense that G.R. Thursby defines the concept of communalism. He feels that the two communities adopt different interpretations of history to express their sense of loss and a feeling of being under threat. The Hindu feeling is summed up as a "dying race", and the Muslim feeling as "backwardness". Such feelings give rise to a survival instinct. The members of the community take actions to preserve and protect their identity and take a confrontationist view vis-à-vis the other group.[6]

The two-nation theory that was propagated during the freedom struggle was a part of this communalist ideology. In fact, it was the minority group that propounded this theory and demanded a separate state for the Muslims. The Hindus were naturally provoked by this demand. The fundamentalists amongst them were encouraged to foster their own unity as a religious group.

Humayun Kabir believed that in a plural and democratic society communalism is inevitable because of clash of interests between minority groups and the majority community.[7] He argued that the birth of democratic institutions created multiple centres of power, with the result that the interest groups got diversified and competition arose among the elites of different communities who tried to invoke communal consciousness. It

5. Ratna Naidu, *Communal Edges to Plural Society: India and Malaysia*, Vikas Publishing House, New Delhi, 1980, p. 87.

6. G.R.Thursby, *Hindu-Muslim Relations in British India: A Study of Controversy, Conflict and Communal Movement in Northern India 1923-1928*, E.J. Brill, Leiden, Netherlands, 1975, p. 2.

7. Humayun Kabir, *Minorities in a Democracy*, K.L. Mukhopadhyay, Calcutta, 1968, p.6.

is the minority consciousness, Kabir surmised, that has caused psychological cleavages and political rifts between the Hindus and Muslims. Minority-majority consciousness has influenced the electoral behaviour and political strategies of the contending parties. Supporting this contention, A. B. Shah called the minorities king-makers.[8] According to Francis Robinson, "the Muslim elite organised themselves in order to secure power and protect its self-interest against the challenges generated by the British rule in India."[9] The Muslims developed this consciousness more pronouncedly compared to other minority groups in India because they received covert encouragement from the British to assert their right. The fact that they were a ruling race prior to the arrival of the British, and that they had a feeling of severe deprivation both politically and economically, contributed to the fostering of communal feelings. Zenab Bano attributes the growth of Muslim consciousness to the Hindu revivalist trend. "Hindu agitation for the adoption of *Devnagri* script was strongly opposed by the Muslims who associated Hindi with the Hindus, and likewise, regarded Urdu as the language of the Muslims. Similarly, Hindu opposition to separate electorates for the Muslims only made the latter more vocal opponents of the Hindus, criticising them as anti-Muslim."[10]

Bipan Chandra identified three conditions for the birth of communalism.[11] These are:

1. People who follow the same religion have common secular interest.

---

8. A.B. Shah, "The Facts of Communalism", *The Secularist*, No.8, December 1970.
9. Francis Robinson, *Separatism among Indian Muslims*, Vikas Publishing House, Delhi, 1975, pp. 345-55.
10. Zenab Bano, *Politics of Communalism: A Politico-Historical Analysis of Communal Riots in Post- Independent India with reference to Gujarat and Rajasthan Riots*, Popular Prakashan, Bombay, 1989, pp.30-31.
11. Bipan Chandra, *Communalism in Modern India*, Vikas Publishing House, New Delhi, 1987, pp.8-9.

2. The secular interests of different religions are dissimilar or divergent from the followers of other religion.
3. When interests of different religions are seen to be incompatible, antagonistic, and hostile.

A number of writers consider communalism as opposed to secularism. They treat communalism as a negative connotation of secularism implying thereby that what is communal is not secular and what is secular is non-communal. Secularism, by contrast, is defined in terms of communal harmony between Hindus and Muslims in India.

Religion has played a major role in creating antagonism and distrust between Hindus and Muslims. In both the communities there are conservatives/traditionalists and the secular-minded modernists. The conservatives amongst both the communities have resisted the forces of modernity and change and yet both have shown an attitude of mutual adjustment as long as religion did not come in their way. However, the urge for the preservation of the distinct religious identity is stronger among the Muslims because of their minority status. They have made extra effort for preserving and deepening their identity by extending communal distinctions in all walks of life.[12] The Muslim attitude of preserving their identity has created a suspicion in the minds of Hindus who question their patriotism and allege their loyalty to Pakistan; interestingly, such allegiance towards Bangladesh is not mentioned although that nation's creation was an extension of the same process that created Pakistan---what is now Bangladesh was originally a part of Pakistan, designated as East Pakistan.

Zenab Bano regards communalism as essentially a political

12. Krishna Gopal, "Communal Issues Revisited", *Times of India*, 10 October 1974.

phenomenon. She believes that "the outcome of communalism in the form of group prejudices, communal contradictions, tensions and riots is due to the struggle for control over the resources of power. Communalism's roots are deep in economic power and domination."[13] The same view is held by Prabha Dixit who regards "communalism as a political doctrine that makes use of religious and cultural differences in achieving political gains."[14]

Asghar Ali Engineer considers communalism as a manifestation of the conflicts of the elite of the community and a strategy to protect their class interests. As an illustration, Engineer quotes the involvement in the pre-partition days of the Muslim elite of the then United Provinces---now Uttar Pradesh---in the Muslim League which was motivated by their desire to defend their privileges. He extends and expands the meaning of communalism by defining it as a "process of ideologisation of interests" and explains the 'why' and 'how' of communal riots. For him, it is the product of transformation of social and economic causation into a religious one.[15]

There are others who ascribe communalism to the colonial form of economy, because full capitalist development was not allowed by the colonial masters and slow development resulted in frustration amongst the relatively deprived and provoked them to fight for their cause. This gave birth to communalism. Others think that communalism is the development of a disproportionately high loyalty to one's caste, tribe or religion

13. Zenab Bano, "A Political Scientist's View of Communalism", as cited in Asghar Ali Engineer and Moin Shakir (ed.), *Communalism in India*, Ajanta Publications, Delhi, 1985, p. 80.
14. Prabha Dixit, *Communalism - A Struggle for Power*, Orient Longman, Delhi, 1974, p. 2.
15. Asghar Ali Engineer, "Communalism: Its Facets and Roots", *Mainstream*, XXIV, June 1986.

as against the normal requirement of pride and loyalty to the nation-state transcending narrow primordial loyalties.[16] In the words of Romila Thapar: "Communalism has to be seen from what it is, an intermixing of ideology and power, where groups aspiring for power use a particular religious ideology to subvert a social order and replace it with an order that is based on sharp differentiation between those who accept the ideology and those who do not. It also places power in the hands of the authors of that ideology."[17]

Rasheeduddin Khan has, however, a different view about communalism. He does not like to equate it with either religion or religiosity. According to him, "it is a process of demeaning religion for narrow and expedient power politics. It is exploitation of religiosity for subverting and fragmenting national identity. Adherence to religion, and religious system is not communalism; exploitation of it is communalism. Using a religious community against other communities and against nation is communalism."[18]

Randhir Singh regards communalism as "an aspect of politics of the ruling classes in a society with a massive feudal-colonial inheritance, deep religious divisions, and undergoing its own historically specific form of capitalist development."[19]

Louis Dumont also considers communalism as a product of

16. K. Subramaniam, "Communalism and Nation-State Building", as cited in Pramod Kumar's *Towards Understanding Communalism*, Centre of Research in Rural and Industrial Development, Chandigarh, 1992, p. 35.
17. Romila Thapar, "Politics of Religious Community", *Seminar*, Vol.365, January, 1992.
18. Rasheeduddin Khan, *Bewildered India: Identity, Pluralism, Discord*, Har Anand Publications, Delhi, 1994, p. 202.
19. Randhir Singh, "Communalism and the Struggle Against Communalism: A Marxist View", as cited in K.N. Panikar (ed.), *Communalism in India: History, Politics and Culture*, Manohar Publications, New Delhi, 1991, p. 124.

interaction between tradition and modernity. Thus, he said: "In communalism, elements of both worlds---political entities of the traditional kind on the one hand, and the modern nation, on the other---are mixed, though the main trend is perhaps modern. Communalism appears as a hybrid, as an intermediary, perhaps a transitory phenomenon. But communalism is fundamentally ambiguous. It can finally appear either as a genuine transition to the nation, or as an attempt on the part of religion to oppose the transformation by allowing for the external appearance of a modern state."[20]

Gyanendra Pandey argues that "in its common Indian usage the word 'communalism' refers to the condition of suspicion, fear and hostility between members of different religious communities. In academic discussions, the term is applied for organised political movements based on proclaimed interests of a religious community usually in response to a real or imaginary threat from the other religious community. It denotes movements that make sectional demands on state policy for a given share in jobs, education and legislative positions; in extreme cases, it may lead to demands for the creation of a new province or state."[21] Following this logic, it can be said that the creation of Pakistan was a culmination of such a process, and the present demands for Khalistan, as well as for the autonomy for Jammu & Kashmir are part of the same extremist positions taken in the name of religion

Pradeep Nayak also holds a similar view. He believes that communalism should be perceived as a state of consciousness and a strategy of mobilisation of a community for a political

20. Cited in Gyanendra Pandey, *The Construction of Communalism in Colonial North India*, Oxford University Press, New Delhi, 1990, p. 3.

21. Gyanendra Pandey, *The Construction of Communalism in Colonial North India*, Oxford University Press, New Delhi, 1990, p. 67.

purpose to form a political community out of religious issues.[22]

In the light of the above definitions, following features of communalism can be culled out:

1. Communalism is associated with religious affiliation.
2. It unites people of a particular religious faith for secular causes, and thus uses religion for political purposes.
3. It arises from a perceived, or even concocted, threat from other religious group.
4. It creates greater in-group solidarity by creating negative stereotypes about the out-group.
5. Communalism expresses itself in violent tensions designed to hurt the other party—riots, arson, and even attack on the religious faith of the other party.
6. It also derives support from the followers of the same faith but belonging to other political regimes. Such external support—not only emotional but also financial, and even in terms of arms, tends to internationalise the conflict and thus goes beyond disrupting internal peace by threatening the very integrity of the nation. Secessionist tendencies exhibited by the extreme form of communalism result in terrorist activities.

Seen in this perspective, communalism in India can be understood as a result of growing mistrust between the two major population groups, namely, the Hindus and the Muslims. At a lower level, communalist tendencies are also seen between the castes and also between practitioners of different sects within one religion. It is, however, interesting that the same kind of occurrence when involves the two religious communities becomes "communal". Sometimes, a personal conflict between the two individuals or families belonging to

22. Pradeep Nayak, *The Politics of Ayodhya Dispute: Rise of Communalism and Future Voting Behaviour*, Commonwealth Publishers, New Delhi, 1993, p. 13.

different communities is ultimately given a colour of a communal conflict as each side gathers more and more supporters for its cause from one's own community. Therefore, there is a need to distinguish between different types of conflict that are referred to as "communal conflicts". How an individual conflict is transformed into a communal conflict depends on the nature of the conflict and the political environment of the locality where it occurs.

Since India is committed to a secular polity, communalism has come to mean "non-secular". While the Constitution of India clearly mentions freedom of religion, some scholars regard every religious activity as anti-secular. The Hindi translation of the word 'secularism' is *dharma-nirapekshata*, that is, religious neutrality. It only means that unlike some other states in the region, such as Pakistan, India does not have a state religion. But it does not imply that the Indian State disallows the practice of religion. In this sense, adherence to a religion, and being religious, or observance of rituals and festivals cannot be regarded as communal. As long as the practitioners of different faiths live in peaceful co-existence, the system of secular polity is not adversely affected. It is only when such peace disappears and disruptive tendencies set in to disturb the harmony and cause a situation of conflict between the different religious communities that communalism surfaces. There could be intended or unintended acts on the part of the "other party" which may lead to a conflict. Sometimes, the interested parties and vested interests may engineer this. Communalism may also emerge when members of a particular community articulate their genuine demand for social justice but is interpreted by the other party as unjust and uncalled for.

However, broadly speaking, the phenomenon of communalism has come to be associated with the strategy of political mobilisation usually perpetuated by the elites of various political parties in their quest for political power. It is a different issue altogether that some parties (e.g., BJP) have gone to a greater extent in using this strategy of political mobilisation which has yielded significant political dividends in course of time, whereas others (e.g., Congress) have used communal tactics for perpetuation of their political power.

There are various factors that can accentuate tensions and still others which could aggravate them. Hence, in order to understand the dynamics of this process, it is necessary to have in-depth studies of the various cases of communal clashes. Much of the literature that exists on this topic is based on normative analyses but there is a continuous necessity for carefully carrying out intensive case studies.

3

Growth of Communalism in India

India has a history of waves of external aggression that initially caused confrontations between the outside aggressors and the indigenous elements. Subsequently, the outsiders got absorbed through the processes of accommodation and assimilation. The principle of co-existence has reigned supreme that helped develop a pluri-cultural, multi-religious society in India. But somewhere, deep in the memory lane, remain the bruises of violent conflict. Even after the resolution of conflicts, and restoration of peace with a new power balance, the memories of the "bad" days continue to linger.

The entire Mughal period that preceded the British colonisation, was a period of constant wars between the expanding Mughal empire and the resisting regional regimes. These wars caused destruction not only of the people and property of the local communities, but also demolition of places of worship and "loot" of valuables. The weaker and vulnerable groups from amongst the conquered populations were also weaned away from their primordial ties of religion through forced or lured "conversions". People may reconcile with the loss of their property but an attack on one's places of worship is rarely forgotten. The religious-minded Hindus carried this grudge all along and worshipped those Hindu kings----such as Shivaji of Maharashtra and Maharana Pratap of Mewar----who put up a strong resistance to the invading Islamic rulers.

When the British overthrew the Muslim rulers, the latter also joined the ranks of the deprived, and united themselves with other sections of the non-Muslim population in a common cause of fighting for the freedom of their adopted motherland. It is a well-known sociological fact that in face of outside threat, people forget their internal differences and put up a common front to save the integrity of the larger entity. It is this sociology of group dynamics that shaped the politics of the Indian freedom struggle, thus bringing the people of different religions and races under one banner to put up a united front against the colonialists. The famous couplet, *Hindu, Muslim, Sikh, Isai; Bharat Mata Sabki Mai* (Hindu, Muslim, Sikh and Christians; all are children of Mother India) sums up the governing ethos of the freedom struggle. Thus, the initial period of British rule brought together people of different faiths and sects against the British. The clarion call for India's freedom from the yoke of colonialism was a call for all to which the entire nation responded positively.

The British, however, knew that the communities within India were divided along lines of religion and language, and that they had a history of internal fights and conflicts. They, therefore, devised the strategy of "divide and rule", by using particularly the communal factors. Thus, it was during the British period that the communal virus spread widely in the Indian body politic and at the instance of the rulers. When the British came to establish their rule over India, their first confrontation was with the Muslim elite class. The superstructure of British imperialism, according to the British, had to be built upon the regimes of dwindling Islamic rule. They, therefore, initiated a process of gradual elimination of the Muslim elites from the centre stage of Indian politics. Simultaneously, they promoted the Hindu aristocracy. The spread of the elite education and the general receptivity of the Hindu elites for such changes paved the way for a new power equation. Hurt by the British, the defeated Muslim elites resisted the modernisation effort and denied their people an exposure to English education. Such deliberate distancing from the forces of change created a new solidarity among them. But it also weakened their power of bargaining.

The establishment of the Indian National Congress in 1885 was a response to the British policy of creating a divide between the Hindus and the Muslims. The aim of the newly established body was to act as a nationalist organisation seeking membership from all sections of the Indian society and putting pressure on the government. It served as an umbrella organisation to provide cover to a variety of interest groups including the Hindu revivalists. In order to receive the widest possible support from diverse religious groups, the Congress adopted a consensual strategy and promoted the concept of 'territorial nationalism'. While leaders from both the communities joined this organisation there were many Muslim leaders who were apprehensive about the role of Hindu leaders in the Congress. They felt that the westernised Hindu elite—who controlled the Congress—would not adequately promote Muslim interests, and may even hurt them. As a consequence, they began to consolidate Muslim support in the country for the protection of the interests of the Muslim community. It was such feeling that led Ghulam-us-Saqlain to propose a separate political organisation for Muslims in the year 1903. He justified this by saying that, "owing to the want of such an organisation, the interests of the Muslim community have already suffered in a variety of ways and are still being trampled under boot."[1] He also dissuaded the Muslims from joining the Congress. It was at this crucial juncture (in 1905) that the Viceroy, Lord Curzon, took the decision to partition the province of Bengal on the communal basis. Notwithstanding the explanation given by the government that the objective of the partition was purely administrative, many regarded this as a step towards creating a gulf between the Hindus and the Muslims. The partition of Bengal, called by the people as *Bang-Bhang*, was violently opposed, particularly by the Hindus. In their view, this act was designed to destroy the cultural integrity of the region where Hindus and Muslims have co-existed for centuries. They argued that people of both the communities inhabited all the parts of the province, and dividing it on the basis of religious concentration was a nefarious tactic of the British government.

The agitators decided to boycott foreign goods and launch a *Swadeshi* (indigenous) movement, that is, to opt for country-made goods and to discard goods coming from abroad, mainly from the United Kingdom. Many Muslims, on the other hand, adopted a pro-government attitude and sought protection from the government against the rioters. Since the Muslims were the beneficiaries of the partition, most of them naturally sided with the government and opposed the predominantly Hindu agitationists. The agitation against the partition of Bengal, thus, took a communal turn. Alongside of the partition of Bengal, the British government also announced its intention to introduce political reforms to give proper representation to different communities in democratic governance.

A delegation of Muslim leaders called on the Viceroy, Lord Minto, at Shimla in October 1906 to request him to introduce

---

1. Francis Robinson, *Separatism among Indian Muslims*, Vikas Publishing House, New Delhi, 1975, pp. 133-38.

the principle of separate representation for Muslims at all levels of government. The Viceroy assured them of full protection of their interests. Encouraged by such a sympathetic response, the Muslims, under the leadership of Agha Khan, decided to form a separate political organisation calling it the All India Muslim League. The League, thus, came into being at Dhaka on 30 December 1906. That was India's first major communal political party in the sense that its membership was confined only to one community, i.e. the Muslims, and its programme was charted for the political and general well-being of the Muslims. Soon, the League set up its branches in various parts of the country. In Aligarh, the branch was established in 1908. Simultaneously, other organisations to propagate Islamic faith were also created. For example, in 1913 the Muslim leaders from Aligarh and Deoband set up in Delhi an institution named *Nizarat-ul-Maarif* (Academy of Quaranic Learning). Similarly, under the headship of Maulana Abdul Bari of Lucknow, an independent society named *Khuddam-i-Kaaba* (Servants of Kaaba) was set up to express the concern of Muslims about their religious places in Central Asia.

The All India Muslim League's overall orientation was in contrast to the Indian National Congress, the membership of which cut across communal lines. Unlike the Muslim League, the Congress was not a communal party of the Hindus; while no Hindu could be a member of the Muslim League, several Muslims remained members of the Congress, and occupied senior leadership positions in it. Of course, as a reaction to the creation of the Muslim League, some Hindu leaders also decided to organise themselves; the United Bengal Hindu Movement and the Punjab Hindu Sabha (set up in 1907) were the first responses from the Hindus in this direction. Eventually, in December 1913, at Allahabad, an All India Hindu Maha Sabha was created. The members of the Sabha were largely Arya Samajists and most of them were also active members of the Congress party.

At its first meeting, the leaders of the Hindu Maha Sabha took pains to clarify that "the Sabha is not a sectarian or denominational one, but an all-embracing movement and does not mean any offence to any other movement, whether Hindu or non-Hindu. It aims to be ardent and watchful in safeguarding the interests of the entire Hindu community in all respects".[2]

Thus, both the Muslim League and the Hindu Maha Sabha were founded to work for the interests of their respective communities. However, as the two organisations grew, they got polarised, taking the shape of two opposite camps. The British encouraged this rift as it adversely affected the Congress unity and thus served the British cause.

By the beginning of the 20th century, the rift between the Hindus and Muslims had widened and the extremists in the two groups had assumed antagonistic postures. The hardened position taken by the leaders of the Muslim League led them to distance from the Congress; as a consequence, the Congress party came to be led mainly by the Hindus. The British and the Muslim League highlighted this development by projecting the Congress as the representative of the Hindu culture and tradition. The observance of *Ganapati* festival and *Shivaji Utsava* promoted by Bal Gangadhar Tilak was interpreted by them as an assertion of Hinduism by the Congress. The agitation against the partition of Bengal was also seen in the same light. At the same time, many Hindu leaders often alluded to the Muslims as "foreigners" and identified nationalism with Hindus. The Muslims, in turn, referred to Hindus as *Kafirs.* But, the nationalist freedom fighters did their best to keep the secular character of the national movement intact, carefully avoiding participation in communal bickerings and promoting

2. Craig Baxter, *The Jan Sangh: A Biography of an Indian Political Party*, University of Pennsylvania Press, Philadelphia, 1969, p. 8.

a feeling of goodwill towards each other.[3]

The British had, however, different motives. Rather than closing the ranks, they wanted this rift to widen so as to further consolidate their grip over the colony. The Morley-Minto Reforms of 1909 that introduced separate electorates on communal lines is a clear proof of this. Under this system, separate constituencies were set up for Muslims from where only Muslim candidates could contest. Such separatism restricted inter-community interaction and turned the legislative bodies into "arenas of communal conflicts".[4]

However, when the British reversed their decision to partition Bengal in December 1911 it came as a rude shock to the Muslims. The Muslim movement received a serious setback. The Muslims also got agitated over the attitude of the British government towards Turkey during the Tripoli and Balkan wars. At the same time, they were puzzled at the sympathy expressed by the national press towards the Muslim brethren in those countries.

The Muslims were in real dilemma: the British backing out from their earlier decision to partition and also acting against the interests of the Muslims in the Middle East on the one hand, and the Indian nationalists supporting the cause of the Turkish people, on the other. They were at bay to decide as to with whom to side with.

It is worth mentioning here that not all the Muslim leaders supported the Muslim League; the nationalists among them saw merit in working with the leaders of the other community. Thus Maulana Azad's *Al-Hilal*[5] and Maulana Mohammad Ali's

3. See Bipan Chandra, *India's Struggle for Independence*, Vikas Publishing House, New Delhi, 1988, p. 410.
4. Ibid., p.419.
5. The Urdu weekly *Al-Hilal* was started by Maulana Azad in 1912 from Calcutta.

Comrade and *Hamdard*[6] pleaded in favour of nationalism. Under the influence of moderates, the constitution of Muslim League was amended at its Lucknow session in March 1913. The League redefined its objectives as:

(i) attainment under the aegis of the British crown of a system of self-government suitable to India through constitutional means by bringing about reforms in the existing system of administration; and

(ii) promotion of national unity.

In December 1915, both the Muslim League and the Indian National Congress held their sessions in Bombay. It is important to note that Madan Mohan Malaviya, Sarojini Naidu and Mahatma Gandhi went to attend the session convened by the Muslim League. The League appointed a Committee to prepare a scheme for unity of Hindus and Muslims in consultation with the Congress. Another session of both the League and the Congress was held at Lucknow in 1916 where the Committee presented its scheme for unity. An agreement, known as Lucknow Pact, was reached between the League and the Congress accepting separate electorates for Muslims and allowing them representation in excess of their proportion of population in the provinces, except in Punjab and Bengal. By accepting the principle of separate electorates, the Congress also became a player in communal politics.

Meanwhile, Abdul Bari launched the Khilafat movement with an All India Central Khilafat Committee in Bombay, and its branches throughout the country.[7] The Muslim League directed its local branches to support the movement. Mahatma

6. Maulana Mohammad Ali founded the *Comrade* (English) and *Hamdard* (Urdu) in 1912 at Delhi.

7. G.R. Thursby, *Hindu-Muslim Relations in British India: A Study of Controversy, Conflict and Communal Movement in Northern India,* E.J. Brill, Leiden, Netherlands, 1975, p. 129.

Gandhi also lent support to the Khilafat movement. In view of the Hindu support to the Khilafat movement Abdul Bari promised to halt cow slaughter.

The year 1921 saw unprecedented cooperation between the two communities. Joint political action was launched for securing *Swaraj*. However, a few violent clashes between the Moplahs---a Muslim group---of Kerala and the Hindus took place, which resulted in their divide. The Non-Cooperation Movement that started as a non-violent protest gave rise to widespread communal riots.[8] It convinced the Hindu revivalists that a rapprochement was rather difficult. Swami Shraddhanand, who was one of the leaders of the Non-Cooperation Movement and who had earlier won the confidence of the Muslims by his bold and courageous actions, was deeply hurt by the Moplah incident. As a reaction, he started the *Shuddhi* movement to reconvert the converted Muslims.[9] The Hindu Maha Sabha, under the leadership of Pandit Madan Mohan Malaviya, supported the *Shuddhi* movement. The Muslim leaders, on the other hand, strongly objected and reacted violently. A series of riots took place in North Indian cities on the issue of conversions. Between 1922 and 1927, as many as 112 riots were reported to have taken place. Swami Shraddhanand was assassinated by a Muslim in 1927. His assassination further added to the antagonism between the two communities.

These events made the Hindu revivalists think of uniting Hindus to preserve their self-esteem. The Hindu Maha Sabha enlarged its membership with its branches proliferating throughout the country. They rallied the Hindus around the slogan: "Hinduism is in danger." It was at this juncture that the Rashtriya Swayamsevak Sangh (RSS) was established (1925).

8. Rajendra Prasad, *India Divided*, Hind Kitabs, Bombay 1946, p. 116.

9. Ibid., p. 117.

The main objective of the RSS was similar to that of the Hindu Maha Sabha, namely, maintenance, protection, and promotion of the Hindu race, Hindu culture and Hindu civilisation for the advancement of the Hindu *Rashtra* (nation).

The nationalist leaders, greatly concerned over the communal problem, made efforts to ease the situation. One suggestion was to abolish the system of separate electorates. Some prominent Muslim leaders met in Delhi in March 1927 to consider this proposal and put four demands before agreeing to a system of joint electorates. These demands were: (i) Sindh be made into a separate province, (ii) the North-West Frontier Province and Baluchistan be treated on the same footing as other provinces, (iii) the proportion of Muslim representation in the Punjab and Bengal be in accordance with their population, and (iv) that their representation should not be less than one-third of the total seats in the central legislature.[10] The Congress appointed a committee under the chairmanship of Moti Lal Nehru to look into the Delhi proposals made by the Muslim League. The Nehru Committee recommended that: (i) India should be a "federation" of linguistic provinces, (ii) provinces should be given autonomy, (iii) elections should be held on the basis of joint electorate, and (iv) seats in central and provincial legislatures be reserved for religious minorities in proportion to their population. The Committee recommended the separation of Sindh from Bombay and suggested constitutional reforms in regard to the North-West Frontier Province.[11]

The Report of the Nehru Committee was placed before an All-Party Convention in December 1928. But, during this time, differences had arisen within the Muslim League. A section of the League and Khilafatists was willing to accept joint

10. Ibid., pp. 120-21.

11. Bipan Chandra, op.cit., p. 423.

electorates and other proposals of the Nehru Report on the condition that the amendments proposed by Jinnah were accepted. Jinnah proposed that (i) the Muslim representation in the central legislature should not be less than one-third; (ii) in the event of adult suffrage not being granted as proposed in the Nehru Report, Punjab and Bengal should have seats on a population basis; and (iii) residuary powers should vest in the provinces. But, the All-Party Convention did not accept these amendments. Moreover, a large section of the League was not willing to give up the provision for separate electorates. The Hindu Maha Sabha also objected to that part of the report which dealt with the Sindh, North-West Frontier Province, Bengal and Punjab. The League thereafter withdrew from the Convention.

Following the failure of the Convention, a Muslim All-Party Conference was convened in Delhi on 31 December 1928. This was presided over by Agha Khan. The Conference passed a resolution making several demands. It asserted that Indian Muslims would not accept any constitution if it was not in conformity with the principles enunciated in the resolution. At this stage, Jinnah formulated a 14-point agenda that included four Delhi proposals, three Calcutta amendments and seven additional points regarding separate electorates and reservation of seats in government services and other governing bodies. This 14-point programme became the basis of the Muslim communalist politics from this time onwards.

The agitation against the Simon Commission and the Civil Disobedience Movement (*Savinay Avagya Andolan)* from 1930 through 1934 swept the entire country with participation from all the communities. Although the Civil Disobedience Movement attracted widespread support from all the communities, yet the chain of Hindu-Muslim riots continued. In 1931, serious Hindu-Muslim riots took place Banaras, Kanpur and other places in the then United Provinces. On 16

August 1932, a Communal Award was announced by MacDonald that accepted all the 14 points advanced by Jinnah. However, efforts for some settlement did succeed. The Hindus, the Muslims and the Sikhs agreed on the appointment of a committee to negotiate an agreed solution of the communal problem. A Unity Conference was held at Allahabad on 3 November 1932. In all, 63 Hindus, 11 Sikhs, 39 Muslims and eight Christians attended it. The Conference appointed a committee of ten persons to work out a feasible solution to communal conflicts. While these efforts were afoot, the British government surprised everyone by its decision to allot 33 per cent of seats to Muslims in the central legislature and to make Sindh a separate province with adequate finances from the Central government.[12]

By this announcement, the British undid the unity efforts made by the secular leadership of the country. Under this new Act of 1935, elections were held in the winter of 1937. In this election, the League lost heavily; it could win only 109 of the 482 seats it had contested. Besides, it also failed to win a majority of seats in any of the four Muslim dominated provinces. This was a terrible blow to a party that claimed to be the sole representative of Indian Muslims. On the other hand, the Congress got majority in seven provinces; independent candidates of Bombay and North-West Frontier Province also decided to align with the Congress thus giving it a clear majority.

Though the Muslim League fought this election in Muslim dominated areas, it suffered heavy losses and failed to get a majority. Greatly embarrassed by the election results, the League decided to concentrate all its efforts to woo the Muslims. For this, it raised a spectre of discrimination against Muslims by the "Hindu" Congress. The Muslim leadership

12. Rajendra Prasad, op.cit., p. 132.

began giving a communal colour to each and every issue----big or small. Frustrated by the defeat, Jinnah even raised objection to the singing of the national song----*Vande Mataram*----saying that it was a Hindu song. For the 15 years that he had been a member of the Congress party he never raised this objection, but suddenly he changed his posture finding it objectionable from the Muslim point of view. It may be pertinent to mention that this song was sung even in all the gatherings during the *Khilafat* agitations with not a single Muslim objecting to it. But when Congress ministries were formed after the 1937 elections defeating the Muslim League, the Muslim leaders made it an issue and a cause for conflict. To remove any misunderstanding, the Congress directed that only the first stanza of *Vande Mataram* should be sung so that any religious reference in the subsequent stanzas may not hurt the feelings of the Muslims. Even then, the League was not satisfied. Then, it started objections to the tri colour flag of the Congress.

The Muslim League demands went on mounting and it became increasingly difficult for the Congress to accommodate all its demands and to reach peaceful settlements. Jinnah now insisted that the League should be recognised as the only representative body of the entire Indian Muslim community and the Congress as the representative body of the Hindus. He wrote to Gandhi on 3 March 1938: "We have reached a stage where no doubt should be left. You recognise the All India Muslim League as the one authoritative organisation of Muslims and, on the other hand, you represent Hindus through the Congress party. Then only we can proceed further and devise a formula for peace."[13]

The Congress found it difficult to concede to any of the communal demands of Jinnah. Jinnah even objected to the inclusion of Muslims in the Peace Committee appointed by the

13. Ibid., p. 145.

Congress. He was bent to use the communal card. In his Presidential Address to the League in 1938, he said: "The high command of the Congress is determined to crush all other communities and cultures in the country and establish a Hindu Raj in the country."[14] On 23 March 1940, at its Lahore session, the Muslim League ultimately adopted the resolution for a separate sovereign country for the Muslims.

The communalists from both parties started playing the communal card after 1937 and indulged in spreading hatred by their provocative and communal speeches. It will be pertinent to mention here a few of them:[15]

> In March 1941, Jinnah said at Aligarh: "Pakistan is not only a practical goal but the only goal if you want to save Islam from complete annihilation from this country."
>
> While commenting on the interim government Jinnah said on 18 August 1946 that the "Congress was a party of upper castes and fascist elements which wanted to rule over the Muslims with the help of British."
>
> While asking the Muslims to vote for the League Jinnah said in 1946: "If we fail to realise our duty today we will be reduced to the status of shudras and Islam will be vanished from India."
>
> Mr Faizul Haq, the premier of Bengal said in 1938 that "Muslim life, limb and property have been lost and blood has freely flowed in Congress provinces. Muslims are leading their life in constant terror and oppressed by Hindus."
>
> Similarly, Mr M.H. Gajdar, a League leader of Sindh said in March 1941 that "the Hindus will have to be eradicated like the Jews in Germany if they did not behave properly."

---

14. As quoted by Bipan Chandra, op.cit., p. 435.
15. Ibid.

Thus, religion was brought into the forefront of propaganda in 1946. The Muslims were asked to vote for the League because, they pleaded that a vote for the League and for a separate state of Pakistan was a vote for Islam. The Muslims were asked to choose between a mosque and a temple. On the other hand, the Hindu communalists did not lag behind in this communal fight. V.D. Savarkar said: "Muslims want to brand the forehead of Hindus and the other non-Muslim section in Hindustan with a stamp of self-humiliation and Muslim domination and to reduce the Hindus to the position of helots in their land." In 1938, he said: "We Hindus are already reduced to be veritable helots throughout our land." M.S. Golwalkar, the chief of the RSS said, in 1939: "If the minority demands are accepted, the Hindu national life will run the risk of being shattered." He attacked the nationalists for hugging the "enemies"---the Muslims, and thus endangering the very existence of the Hindus. He further asked the Muslims and the non-Hindu people in India to adopt the Hindu culture and language, learn to respect Hindu religion, and entertain no ideas but those of glorification of Hindu race and culture. He wrote: "We Hindus are at war at once with the Muslims, on the one hand, and the British, on the other". Hindu leaders also warned the people that Hinduism is in danger.

The growth of feelings of hatred among both the communities led to serious acrimony and riots. It must, however, be said that communal conflicts involving the two communities have a long history. Even during the Mughal period such clashes occurred, particularly when their religious sensitivities were hurt. But, the rulers made efforts to resolve such crises through consensus. These riots assumed a political colour only after the advent of the British. The frequency of their occurrence also increased. It is striking that while between 1730 and 1924, only 39 riots were reported which took place mostly in 28 North Indian cities, as many as 101 riots occurred between 1925 and 1927. The peak of communal frenzy reached between 1946 and 1948 when violent riots occurred in Calcutta and Nawakhali.

Available reports suggest that the first riot took place in Ahmedabad in 1730. The immediate cause of the dispute was a trivial one. The Muslim residents of a neighbourhood asked their Hindu neighbours not to observe the festival of Holi that requires lighting a bonfire and then throwing of colours on each other. Disregarding the suggestion, the Hindus went ahead with the ceremony of bonfire. The irritated Muslims retorted by slaughtering a cow in front of a Hindu house next day. The cow slaughter understandably angered the Hindus who attacked the Muslim houses of the locality. In this confrontation, one of the Muslims was killed. The Muslim retaliation was inevitable; this resulted in a communal riot in which a number of persons---both amongst Hindus and Muslims---were killed and there was extensive damage to the property. Some leaders from both the sides appealed to the government to intervene to stop the bloodshed. Another major incident of riot is reported in *The District Gazetteer of Banaras* (now renamed Varanasi) that occurred in 1809. This was on the issue of a mosque built by Mughal Emperor Aurangzeb on the site of an old temple. Most riots upto 1920s were caused by similar factors.

Table 1 lists the riots that took place between 1730 and 1924---in 194 years---in various cities of India.

The rising incidence of communal riots and the separatist stance taken by the Muslim leadership led people to advance the "two-nation theory". Both the Hindu Maha Sabha and the Muslim League were of the view that Hindus and Muslims were the two nations that could not co-exist in one country. The Hindu Maha Sabha passed a resolution in 1937 accepting the two-nation theory proposed by the Muslim League. Bhai Paramanand, a Maha Sabha leader, wrote in 1938: "I agree with

Table 1
Places where Communal Riots Took Place (1730-1924)

1730	Ahmedabad
1806	Manunath (Mau)
1809	Banaras
1813	Mubarakpur
1834	Mubarakpur
1837	Bareli
1842	Mubarakpur
1843	Lucknow
1853	Lucknow
1855	Lahore and Karnal
1856	Lucknow
1871-72	Bareli
1886	Delhi
1889	Dera Ghazikhan
1891	Palakod
1893	Azamgarh and Bombay
1904	Mubarakpur
1910	Peshawar
1911	Bombay
1912	Ayodhya (Faizabad)
1913	Agra
1917	Shahabad
1918	Kartarpur, Saharanpur and Calcutta
1921	Malegaun
1922	Multan
1923	Lahore, Amritsar and Saharanpur
1924	Allahabad, Calcutta, Delhi, Gulbarga, Kahat, Lucknow and Nagpur

Mr Jinnah that there are two nations in the country. The Congress theory of building up a common nationality falls to the ground. The situation has only two solutions. One is the partition of the country and the second is to allow a Muslim state to grow within the state." Thus, both the communal forces----Muslim or Hindu----supported the idea, which resulted in the partition of the country on religious grounds in 1947.

The partition of the country unleashed pent up emotions amongst both the Hindu and Muslim zealots. The euphoria of freedom led to violent clashes between the two taking a toll of innocent lives on both the sides. The partition involved mass migrations and loss of property and people. It greatly hurt Mahatma Gandhi, the Messiah of Hindu-Muslim unity who never wanted the partition of the country and was prepared to sacrifice even his life to keep the integrity of the nation. He tried his best to control the communal riots. He went to Bengal and began fasting in a riot-torn area. His fast finally brought some sense and cooled down the fanatics. But he was unfortunately assassinated by a Hindu fanatic, Nathu Ram Godse, on 30 January 1948 in Delhi while going for his regular evening prayer. Soon after Gandhi's assassination, RSS and Hindu Maha Sabha were banned.

"After the partition, Jawaharlal Nehru and Liaquat Ali, Prime Ministers of India and Pakistan respectively, met in Delhi and signed an agreement known as Delhi Pact on 8 April 1950 affirming the intention of their respective governments to uphold the rights of minorities, to facilitate the movement of migrants and to restore communal harmony in the two Bengals----East Bengal which went to Pakistan, as East Pakistan, and West Bengal, which remained as part of India."[16] Disapproving this Pact, Syama Prasad Mukherjee resigned from Nehru's government and eventually launched a new political party by the name of Bharatiya Jan Sangh, with support from the RSS, on 21 October 1951. While declaring that the party

16. B.D. Graham, *Hindu Nationalism in Indian Politics: The Origin and Development of the Bharatiya Jana Sangh*, Cambridge University Press, New York, 1990, p.23.

would not recognise minority or majority based on religion, it recommended firm policies for dealing with Pakistan.

It must here be said that the assassination of Mahatma Gandhi in 1948 brought about a change in the attitude of the people on the communal question. The Hindu communal elements got isolated. The period between 1950 and 1960 may be called as a decade of communal peace and harmony. However, the first major communal riots occurred in Jabalpur in 1961 between two *bidi* manufacturers, one Hindu and the other Muslim. On 27 December 1963 the theft of a holy relic of the Prophet from the Hazratbal Mosque in Kashmir caused serious riots in Khulna (now in Bangladesh) from where many Hindu families fled to India. As a reaction to this, serious riots broke out in Calcutta, Jamshedpur, Rourkela and Ranchi in 1964 in which hundreds of people were killed.[17]

The Muslim leadership was greatly perturbed by this outburst of communal riots. They thought that the creation of Pakistan jeopardised the prospects of Muslims who decided to stay in India. In order to protect the interests of the Muslims and to express their loyalty to the democratic and secular principles of the Constitution of Independent India *Jamiyat-al-Ulama-i-Hind,* which was set up in 1919, was re-energised in 1948 to "chalk out the path to be traversed by the community for reconstruction (and to march) shoulder to shoulder with members of other communities inhabiting the country."[18] However, it worked to defend Muslim Personal Law and oppose any attempt by the state to change or interfere with it. As against this, *Jamaat-i-Islami*---which came into being in 1941---pursued a more communal agenda. With its fundamentalist overtones, it shared with the *Jamiyat-al-Ulama-i-*

17. Asghar Ali Engineer, *Communal Riots in Post-Independent India*, Sangam Books, Bombay, 1984, p.53.
18. Maulana Asrarul Haque Qasimi, *The Community in Retrospect*, Delhi, n.d., p.1.

Hind the goal of preserving the *Shariat* for Muslims. *Anjuman-e-Taraqqi-e-Urdu* became a leading organisation in India, especially in Uttar Pradesh and Bihar, supporting the cause of Urdu language. Several other organisations also came up at regional levels.

In 1964, S.M. Faridi and Syed Mohammad, ministers in Nehru's cabinet, took initiative in forming *Majlis-e-Mushawarat*, a consultative body of various Muslim groups and political parties to secure adequate Muslim representation in parliament to preserve Muslim character of the Aligarh Muslim University and to prevent parliament from interfering in Muslim Personal Law. The formation of Majlis-e-Mushawarat raised, however, some doubts as to whether this was another attempt by Muslims to create yet another Pakistan. From the very beginning Bharatiya Jan Sangh (BJS) raised the issue of Kashmir and focused on the problem of the refugees who were forced to flee from Pakistan. They argued for a tough policy towards Pakistan. Because of this, and also because of the total support given it by the RSS, BJS was regarded as an anti-Muslim organisation. This feeling was further reinforced when the party asked for a Uniform Civil Code. The Muslims reacted very strongly and formed the Muslim Personal Law Board in the late 1960s to protect their Shariat Law. The Congress government assured the Muslims that it would not interfere in their personal law. This was seen by the BJS as an appeasement tactic of the Congress. It decried the Nehruvian secularism as "pseudo-secularism", because it was favouring people of one religion while neglecting the claims of the majority religion. Comparing the fate of the Hindus in Pakistan, who constituted a small minority there, and the prominence of Islam in the governance of the country, the leaders of the Jan Sangh felt that there was no need to show special favours to the Muslims who had opted to claim a separate state for themselves, and who have no regard for the people belonging to other religions. They also suspected the Muslims of India as having extra-territorial loyalties with Pakistan harming India's interests.

Another wave of communal violence swept the country in 1967 and continued till 1970: Ranchi (1967), Karimganj (1968), Meerut (1968), Ahmedabad (1969). In the 1960s, the communal riots were restricted to towns and cities only and the number of persons killed was also small. In Uttar Pradesh alone, during 1968-1971 a total of 202 riots took place.

Following Table 2, taken from Rasheeduddin Khan's *Bewildered India*, gives the enumeration of Hindu-Muslim riots since 1950.[19]

Table 2

Communal Riots between 1950 and 1992

Year	*No. of Riots*	*Year*	*No. of Riots*
1950-63	341	1980	427
1964-68	289	1981	319
1969	519	1982	474
1970	521	1983	404
1971	321	1984	456
1972	240	1985	50
1973	242	1986	764
1974	248	1987	711
1975	205	1988	611
1976	169	1989	79
1977	188	1990	27
1978	230	1991	29
1979	304	1992 (June)	7

The data show that over a period of forty years, a total of 8175 riots took place in India giving an average of 204 riots per

19. Rasheeduddin Khan, *Bewildered India: Identity, Pluralism, Discord*, Har Anand Publications, Delhi, 1994, p. 223.

year. It is, however, important to note that the first twenty years of Indian independence were relatively peaceful as during that period, and particularly between 1950 and 1968, only 630 riots took place, making an average of 38 riots per year. The years when more than 400 riots took place were: 1969 (519), 1970 (521), 1980 (427), 1982 (474), 1983 (404), 1984 (456), 1986 (764), 1987 (711), and 1988 (611). After this period, there was a sudden fall; the year 1991 saw only 29 riots, and up to June 1992, only seven riots took place---an astonishingly small number.

We may examine yet another source. P. R. Rajgopal, in his study, *Communal Violence in India* (Uppal, New Delhi, 1987) has recounted the frequency and casualties of communal incidents between 1954 and 1985. Rajgopal has listed all the incidents and not just riots, with the result that the number of incidents is much larger than the above table. According to Rajgopal, the increase in communal incidents in this period of thirty years has been six-fold from 84 in 1954 to 525 in 1985, with a peak of 1,070 in 1964---indeed an unduly large number in that year, jumping from 61 in 1963, and climbing down to 173 in 1965. But, after 1965, the number went constantly rising, reaching 525 in 1985. What is more interesting is the fact that despite a large number of riots in 1964, the number of persons killed and injured then was relatively small---in 1964, 1919 persons were killed and another 2,053 were injured; as against this, in 525 riots in 1985 (note that in the official statistics cited in the previous table, there is enumeration of only 50 riots), 325 persons were killed and 3,665 were injured. These details are given in Table 3.

A careful study of the data provided by Rajgopal suggests that most of the incidents of communal violence have occurred in six states, namely, Andhra Pradesh, Bihar, Gujarat, Maharashtra, Rajasthan, and Uttar Pradesh. What is more interesting is the fact that two states which suffered terrible

Table 3

Frequency and Casualties of Communal Incidents (1954-1985)

Year	No. of Incidents	Persons Killed	Persons Injured
1954	84	34	512
1955	75	24	457
1956	82	35	575
1957	58	12	316
1958	40	7	369
1959	42	41	1344
1960	26	14	262
1961	92	81	593
1962	60	43	348
1963	61	26	489
1964	1070	1919	2053
1965	173	34	758
1966	144	45	467
1967	198	251	880
1968	346	133	1309
1969	519	673	2702
1970	528	298	1607
1971	321	103	1263
1972	240	69	1056
1973	242	72	1318
1974	248	87	1123
1975	205	33	890
1976	169	39	794
1977	188	36	1122
1978	230	110	1853
1979	304	261	2379
1980	421	372	2691
1981	319	196	2631
1982	470	238	3025
1983	500	1143	3652
1984	476	445	4836
1985	525	328	3665

Source: P.R. Rajgopal, op.cit., pp.16-17.

communal holocaust in 1947, viz. Punjab and West Bengal, have remained peaceful in this regard. There are also indications that most of these riots occurred in urban metropolitan areas; in terms of the place of origin of the riots, 90 per cent cases were reported to have taken place in the cities.

While these figures give an impression of increasing communal violence over the last five decades, there is another way of looking at them as suggested by Ashis Nandy in the recently published study titled, *Creating A Nationality*. The authors compare these data with that of the United States and come to the conclusion that these "casualty figures... do not add up to the total number of homicides in a respectable North American metropolitan city. Though in recent times these figures have sometimes risen dramatically---1990 and 1992, for instance, were particularly bad years---the Indian figures still remain remarkably small when viewed in the context of the nearly 900 million who inhabit the country. For example, the other large, multi-ethnic, open society, the United States, though one-third of India in population, had in 1990 more than 30,000 cases of homicide (about twenty times the number of people killed in communal violence in India)."[20] The authors regard that there is an "over-concern" with communal violence because of the over-concern of the national media with communal violence that is related by them to the ideology of communalism. Nandy and his co-authors think the other way: all inter-communal conflicts are not caused by communalism. This is, however, not to say that communalism does not inspire violence and cause communal conflicts.

In this context, it is important to note that after the partition, the Muslim leaders changed their demand profile. The new demands related to their cultural and educational

20. Ashis Nandy, Shikha Trivedi, Shail Mayaram and Achyut Yagnik, *Creating A Nationality*, Oxford University Press, Delhi, 1995, p. 9.

rights such as official status for Urdu language, preservation of Muslim Personal Law, job reservation, and a minority status for the Aligarh Muslim University. The opposition to these demands came, quite understandably, from the Bharatiya Jan Sangh.

In the 1970s the country witnessed once again a spate of serious riots: Bhiwandi and Jalgaon (1970), Meerut (1974), Delhi (1976), Muzaffarnagar (1976), Sultanpur (1977), Aligarh (1979) and Jamshedpur (1979).[21] Analysing these events, Asghar Ali Engineer concluded that these riots were caused by different set of factors than the pre-independence riots. A variety of local factors, including conflicting commercial interests, were responsible for these riots that generally took place in middle-sized towns and cities. After independence, the root of this Hindu-Muslim tension was not the issue of cow slaughter or playing music before the mosques. The trouble spots were the places where the Muslim craftsmen were working under Hindu entrepreneurs.[22] Some were, of course, related to inter-religious marriages, which were given a communal colour. According to Zoya Hasan, instances of increasing economic competition are quite numerous in certain areas of Uttar Pradesh. Here Muslims have come to occupy a relatively influential position in the economic and political life of the region that has seemingly threatened the hegemony of existing Hindu commercial groups.[23]

Although several Muslim organisations came up, after independence, to defend Muslim interests, they could not contain the occurrence of communal riots that continue to be an annual feature. But, the period 1970-79 was a quieter period

21. Rasheeduddin Khan, op. cit., p.222.

22. Asghar Ali Engineer (ed.), *Communal Riots in Post-Independent India,* pp. 30-31.

23. Zoya Hasan, "Communalism and Communal Violence in India", in Asghar Ali Engineer (ed.), *Communal Riots in Post-Independent India,* p. 75.

as compared to the previous period of 1964-70. The average number of riots came down from 425 to 234 during this period (1972-79). In the following period, the situation again deteriorated, with the number of riots rising to 440 between 1979 and 1988.

During the Emergency, imposed by Indira Gandhi, no riots took place in India. But Muslims are alleged to have suffered a lot due to excesses committed during that period, particularly in regard to forced vasectomy operations as part of aggressive family planning campaign by Indira Gandhi's son Sanjay Gandhi. It is mainly due to this that the Muslims are said to have shifted their loyalties in the post-Emergency era from the Congress to the newly formed Janata Party in the 1977 elections. This was the time when Jan Sangh also joined the Janata Party. During the Janata regime Shahi Imam of Jama Masjid emerged as a strong Muslim leader. Many Hindus did not like this. The erstwhile Jana Sangh leaders exploited the sentiment of Hindus by opting out of that alliance and forming a new party in the name of Bharatiya Janata Party. The communal problem once again resurfaced and there were riots in Jamshedpur, Aligarh and Varanasi. Muslims suffered a lot in these riots.

When Janata Party fell from power, the Muslims went back to the Congress fold and voted *en bloc* to the Congress party that won the 1980 elections. However, such shifting of loyalties created suspicion in the mind of Indira Gandhi who thought that she could no longer trust and depend on the Muslim vote any more. By this time the problems in Kashmir, Assam and Punjab had already started and the regional parties of these border states where Muslims were in a majority started challenging her. The average Hindu was also perturbed by the growing tensions in the border states. Indira Gandhi sensed the pulse of the people and tried to woo the emerging Hindu middle classes. In the elections of Jammu & Kashmir Legislative

Assembly she played openly the Hindu card and won the elections. Though she won the 1980 election, election results revealed that Muslims in the North had once again tilted towards Janata Party and Lok Dal. Similarly, when the Congress lost Assembly elections in Karnataka and Andhra Pradesh in 1983, the search for a new electoral strategy began. On the other hand, the Jan Sangh constituents of the erstwhile Janata regime also started rethinking their strategy after suffering humiliating defeat in the 1980 elections. Owing to the surfacing of their hitherto ideological differences vis-à-vis the Janata Party, the Jan Sangh constituents finally laid the foundation of the formation of a new political entity having a different and separate ideology of its own in the form of Bharatiya Janata Party (BJP) in 1980. The Congress party projected itself as the sole protector of the national integrity by openly playing the Hindu card. Thereafter, both Congress and BJP started consolidating the Hindu vote bank. And communalism appeared to them as the most convenient tool in their quest for political power. This resulted in disastrous consequences for the national polity in general and Uttar Pradesh in particular, especially in the decade of 1980s.

The Shah Bano Controversy

At this time, a major controversy arose over the issue of Muslim Personal Law. This related to a Supreme Court judgment in favour of Shah Bano who sought the help of the court to receive maintenance grant from her husband who had divorced her.

After being divorced by her husband, Mohammad Ahmad Khan, Shah Bano went to the Madhya Pradesh High Court seeking its help in getting maintenance allowance from her former husband. The court ordered the payment. Against this judgment, Shah Bano's husband filed a petition in the Supreme

Court. The Supreme Court delivered its judgment upholding the High Court judgment and felt that section 125 of the Criminal Procedure Code, which makes it obligatory on husbands to make provision for their divorced wives if they do not have any other means of sustenance, or until they remarry or die, should be equally applicable to the Muslim divorcee women. This section, in their view, was applicable to the Muslim husbands also. Before pronouncing this judgment, the Supreme Court had consulted the text of the holy *Quran* in its standard translations and also the commentaries on it by well-known Muslim authorities published by the Board of Islamic Publications, Delhi.

It may be said here that Shah Bano's case was not the first one on which the Supreme Court has given a verdict favouring the claim of a Muslim divorcee for a maintenance grant from her previous husband. Earlier, in the cases of Tahira Bai vs. Ali Husain Firduli Chothia and Fazumbi vs. Khader Ali in 1970, the then Supreme Court Judge, Mr V.R. Krishna Iyer, had also asked the husbands of the divorcee Muslim women to pay maintenance grant, under section 125 of the Criminal Procedure Code. In those instances, no one questioned the judgment of the apex court. But Shah Bano's case provoked great turmoil and protest, introducing political angle to a social and humanitarian question. The All India Muslim Personal Law Board (AIMPLB), Jamait-ul-ulema, Jamait-e-Islami, leaders of the Indian Union Muslim League, Majlis-e-Mushawarat and the Janata Party leader Shahabuddin strongly objected to this judgement and described it as gross interference in the Muslim Personal Law. In their view, the Supreme Court had no right to interpret the holy *Quran*.[24] Thus, the Supreme Court was held guilty on two counts: first, it had interfered in the Muslim

---

24. Asghar Ali Engineer (ed.), *The Shah Bano Controversy*, Orient Longman Ltd., Hyderabad, 1987, p. 89.

Personal Law, and secondly it had tried to interpret the holy book.

The Supreme Court verdict was, in fact, perceived by the Muslims as an attack on their *Shariat* (Islamic) law. The AIMPLB and other Muslim organisations launched a countrywide agitation against the judgment and mounted pressure on the government to have it withdrawn. Conferences and protest rallies were held at different places. There were big demonstrations by the Muslims throughout the country. It was the biggest ever protest by the Muslims in post-independent India. Some Muslim leaders believed that their identity was at stake and thus they revived the Muslim Majlis and Majlis-e-Mushawarat. This served the cause of uniting the Muslims and bringing them under one banner in the name of religion. Of course, it must be said that not all Muslims shared this view.

Analysing the happenings related to the Shah Bano controversy, Asghar Ali Engineer attributed such response on the part of the Muslims to their sense of insecurity that was caused by a series of events preceding the Shah Bano case. The events that nurtured the feeling of their insecurity were:

1. the Meenakshipuram episode of 1981 and the virulent anti-Muslim propaganda launched by the Vishwa Hindu Parishad (VHP) following it;
2. the case for banning the holy *Quran* filed in the Calcutta High Court;
3. the ban imposed by the Department of Archaeology on prayers in certain historical mosques on the plea of protecting the historical monuments; and
4. the antagonistic campaign by the VHP for liberating Ramjanmabhumi and some other temples in Uttar Pradesh.

All these factors affected the Muslim psyche and provoked an equally virulent reaction among them. Amidst such atmosphere when the Supreme Court delivered the judgment in the Shah Bano case, the Muslims thought that this was yet another instance of undermining their religious identity. The Muslim leaders took advantage of this growing sense of insecurity and organised nationwide protests. It was continuously hammered into the Muslim mind that the divine *Shariat* was in danger and that it was the sacred duty of every Muslim to protect it. A huge rally was organised in Delhi which was addressed, among others, by the Shahi Imam who used venomous language to denounce the attacks on Muslim religion and culture, and expressed his fears that such acts will further alienate the Muslims and make them more antagonistic.

The judgment also provided the Muslim leaders an opportunity to retain their leadership and to emphasise the distinctive identity of the Muslim community. They used this to reinforce the Muslim political identity and to organise them around a common symbol. As Shahabuddin wrote: "Ours is not a communal fight. It only amounts to resisting the unacceptable process of assimilation. We want to keep our identity at all costs".[25]

The judgment affected the political clout of those Muslim leaders who belonged to the Congress. For example, the General Secretary of the Jamiat-e-Ulema-i-Hind, Maulana Asrarul Haque Quasmi, was badly defeated as a Congress candidate by Syed Shahabuddin of the Janata Party in the Kishanganj (Bihar) by-election for the Lok Sabha held in December 1985. Even in Assam elections Muslim voters distanced themselves from the Congress.

Fearing further electoral reverses, the Rajiv Gandhi government introduced a bill in the parliament in February 1986 to exempt Muslims from the purview of section 125 of the

25. *Mainstream*, 10 May 1986, p. 33.

Criminal Procedure Code. This bill was adopted on 5 May 1986 despite strong protests from the opposition parties and several non-political and progressive organisations. The Hindu religious forces saw the government move to nullify the judgment as "capitulation to the Muslim forces". They felt that the government had clearly gone back from its duty to uphold the judiciary and the constitution. Some even went to the extent of saying that the government had subverted the constitution under electoral compulsion.[26] Even a prominent Muslim leader in the cabinet of Rajiv Gandhi, Arif Mohammad Khan, resigned in protest against the passage of the bill.

The leaders of both the communities were, thus, able to mobilise public opinion on this issue and aggravate the situation. The Vishwa Hindu Parishad in Uttar Pradesh used this occasion to reorganise itself with the induction of some renowned intellectuals and former civil servants to impress upon the government the desirability of having a Uniform Civil Code. Their leaders argued that the proposed bill goes against the cherished values of secular India.

26. Pradeep Nayak, op.cit., pp. 30-31.

4

Uttar Pradesh Scene in the 1980s

The phenomenon of communalism—a manifestation of Hindu-Muslim animosity—got consolidated in post-independent India. The success of the British in creating a rift between the two communities, and in dividing the country into two separate nations, left a feeling of ill-will and of suspicion in the minds of both the communities. The Hindus felt cheated, and found it difficult to accept the fact of partition. The Muslims, particularly those who left the country to join Pakistan, had a feeling of euphoria, and a satisfaction of achieving a long-cherished goal. They were also hopeful of getting a better treat in the new-found homeland. Those Muslims who were left behind in India were caught between two contradictory feelings. They were happy to attain the freedom from the British and also to be able to stay at the place of their origin rather than being thrown out as refugee to the newly created State; at the same time, they also had a sense of insecurity, and were afraid of a Hindu backlash as if to take revenge on them for the atrocities committed by their co-religionists against the Hindus in Pakistan. They had apprehensions of being discriminated against. The common feeling among many of them was that as Pakistan was a Muslim state, the remainder of India would become a Hindu state that would not tolerate the presence of other religious groups, particularly the Muslims. The point is not the reality of this perception; it is this perception that shaped the reality of their behaviour.

Whether it was the case of giving equal status to Urdu vis-à-vis Hindi, or the concept of separate electorate for Muslims, or the depiction of the Congress as a Hindu organisation or similar other appeasing tactics adopted by the British to favour the minorities---all contained the "seeds of discontent, hatred and bellicosity" between the two communities. The seeds of acrimony between the Hindus and the Muslims sown by the British produced a harvest of communalism on both the sides; the politicians exploited these attitudes with renewed zeal and vigour in different forms. The exploitation of the religious sentiments of the two communities for political gains was quite prominent in the state of Uttar Pradesh. Being the largest state, and having a unique combination of Hindu-Muslim population, the state became a hot bed of communal politics in the country.

Uttar Pradesh: Demographic Profile

Uttar Pradesh has a large population of 139,112,287 with a literacy rate of only 41.6 per cent, according to the Census of 1991.[1] Areawise also it is fourth in the country. The state has the largest Muslim population of 24,109,684 constituting 17.33 per cent of the total population. The annual rate of growth of the Muslim population during the decade 1981-91 was 3.65 per cent. The following table shows the distribution of population by religion in 1981 and 1991.[2]

1. *Census of India*, 1991, Series No.1, Paper 1 of 1995, Religion.
2. Ibid.

Table 1

Hindu and Muslim Population in India and Uttar Pradesh, 1981-1991

Unit	*1981*	*% of Total Population*	*1991*	*% of Total Population*	*% Growth*
India	665,287,849	100	834,883,012	100	+ 23.79
Hindu	549,724,717	83.09	687,646,721	82.41	+22.78
Muslim	75,571,514	11.73	101,596,057	12.12	+32.76
Uttar Pradesh	110,862,013	100	139,112,287	100	+25.48
Hindu	92,365,968	83.31	113,712,829	81.74	+23.11
Muslim	17,657,735	15.93	24,109,684	17.33	+36.54

The Census data reveal that, as of 1991, the Hindus constitute 82.41 per cent and the Muslims 12.12 per cent of the population; in the ten years 1981-91, while the proportion of Hindu population has declined, that of the Muslims has increased. In Uttar Pradesh, this is more prominent: the Hindu proportion has come down from 83.31 per cent in 1981 to 81.74 per cent in 1991; as against this, the Muslim proportion has increased from 15.93 to 17.33 per cent. In terms of actual numbers, the Muslim population in Uttar Pradesh has registered an increase of 36.54 per cent compared to 23.11 per cent in the case of the Hindus.

Because of the partition of the country, the demographic composition of India has greatly changed after 1947. In 1941, Hindus and Muslims constituted 69.5 per cent and 24.28 per cent respectively of the total population; this composition changed to 84.98 and 11.10 per cent respectively in 1951. In later years, this proportion has continually changed with a rise in the proportion of the Muslim population (see Table 2).

The Muslim population in Uttar Pradesh is constantly showing an upward trend. In 1971, it was 15 per cent of the total population; in 1981 it was 15.93 per cent; and in 1991, it had gone up to 17.33 per cent.

Table 2
Decennial Growth of Hindu and Muslim Populations

Period	*Census Year*	*% Growth (Hindus)*	*% Growth (Muslims)*
Undivided India	1881	75.1	19.97
	1891	74.2	20.41
	1901	72.9	21.88
	1911	71.7	22.39
	1921	70.7	23.23
	1931	70.7	23.49
	1941	69.5	24.28
After Partition	1951	84.98	11.10
	1961	83.51	10.70
	1971	82.72	11.21
	1981	82.79	11.73
	1991	82.00	12.12

Uttar Pradesh has a relatively higher percentage of the Muslim population. The Muslims constitute, according to the 1991 census, 17.33 per cent of the population of the state of Uttar Pradesh, which is higher by 5.21 percentage points of the all-India figure. In 52, out of the 63, districts in the state, Muslim population is more than 5 per cent. There are 16 districts where the Muslims constitute more than 20 per cent.

The entire state is divided into seven administrative regions, which are further divided into districts. Table 3 lists the regions and the districts with Muslim populations as enumerated in the censuses of 1981 and 1991.

The sixteen districts with high percentage of the Muslim populations, according to the 1991 census enumeration, as shown in the table, are: Rampur (47.95%), Moradabad (42.70%), Bijnor (40.35%), Saharanpur (36.12%), Muzaffarnagar (34.52%),

Table 3

List of Districts of U.P. with Percentage of Muslim Population (1981-1991 Census)

	Regions and Districts	*1981*	*1991*
1.	*Uttarakhand*		
	1. Uttar Kashi	0.38	0.90
	2. Tehrigarhwal	0.48	0.83
	3. Garhwal	2.11	2.27
	4. Chamoli	0.47	0.72
	5. Pithoragarh	0.40	0.50
	6. Almora	0.58	0.64
	7 Nainital	12.92	15.23
2.	*Rohilkhand*		
	1.Bijnor	39.48	40.35
	2.Moradabad	38.07	42.70
	3.Rampur	47.22	47.95
	4.Badaun	19.12	20.66
	5.Bareli	27.15	32.69
	6.Pilibhit	21.12	23.13
	7.Shahjahanpur	16.56	17.57
3.	*Oudh*		
	1.Kheri	16.50	18.07
	2.Sitapur	17.64	17.37
	3.Hardoi	10.84	12.58
	4.Unnao	10.68	10.66
	5.Lucknow	19.67	19.66
	6.Raebareli	10.18	11.35
	7.Pratapgarh	10.93	13.25
	8.Sultanpur	12.95	12.94
	9.Faizabad	12.48	13.39
	10.Barabanki	20.45	21.66
	11.Bahraich	25.02	29.92
	12.Gonda	22.48	25.36
	13.Banda	5.51	6.36
4.	*Poorvanchal*		
	1. Basti	16.65	16.51
	2. Sidharthnagar	26.37	28.76

Contd...

Contd...

3. Gorakhpur	8.84	8.09
4. Maharajganj	14.32	15.89
5. Deoria	20.72	20.18
6. Mau.	17.63	17.91
7. Azamgarh	11.96	13.01
8. Ballia	5.33	6.04
9. Ghazipur	10.08	10.07
10. Varanasi	10.45	12.84
11. Jaunpur	8.34	9.74
12. Sonbhadra	4.42	4.94
13. Mirzapur	6.04	6.98
5. *Lower Doab*		
1. Allahabad	12.77	12.94
2. Fatehpur	12.86	12.57
3. Kanpur Nagar	17.79	17.80
4. Kanpur Dehat	6.70	6.91
5. Etawah	6.34	6.63
6. Farrukhabad	12.64	14.17
7. Mainpuri	4.15	5.09
8. Firozabad	10.78	10.76
9. Etah	10.46	11.32
6. *Bundelkhand*		
1. Hamirpur	6.06	7.28
2. Lalitpur	2.11	2.74
3. Jhansi	8.40	8.42
4. Jalaun	8.21	9.27
7. *Upper Doab*		
1. Agra	9.83	10.97
2. Mathura	6.39	8.12
3. Aligarh	13.17	14.63
4. Bulandshahar	19.37	19.78
5. Ghaziabad	21.17	21.16
6. Meerut	25.30	27.49
7. Muzaffarnagar	28.72	34.52
8. Saharanpur	33.17	36.12
9. Haridwar	28.30	30.07
10. Dehradun	8.32	9.63

Bareli (32.69%), Hardwar (30.07%), Bahraich (29.92%), Siddharthnagar (28.76%), Meerut (27.49%), Gonda (25.36%), Pilibhit (23.13%), Barabanki (21.66%), Ghaziabad (21.16%), Deoria (20.18%), and Badaun (20.66%).

Of the above 16 districts, six fall in the Rohilkhand region, five in Upper Doab region, three in Awadh (Oudh), and two in Poorvanchal. Rohilkhand, thus, has the largest Muslim population.

In general, there is high concentration of Muslims in urban areas (28.48%), whereas in rural areas, they constitute only 13.18 per cent. Comparative figures for the Hindus are: 69.63 per cent in urban areas and 86.31 per cent in rural areas.

Muslim Organisations in Uttar Pradesh

Uttar Pradesh, which was known during the British period as United Provinces, occupies a unique place in the history of Indian Muslims. All major national level Muslim institutions have their headquarters here and it is from here that the secessionist ideas spread to other Muslim majority provinces of Punjab, Bengal, Sindh and the North-West Frontier Province. The state has a long history of Hindu-Muslim conflict. It had been a breeding ground for Muslim separatism.

The Muslims of Uttar Pradesh, during the British rule,were in a dominant position. They were educated, well-off and more advanced than the Hindus. Prior to the arrival of the British, they had ruled the various parts of the province as Nawabs and landlords. The deprivations suffered by them at the hands of the British led them to join the Hindus to put up a fight to oust the British; but as the prospects of getting independence improved, the Muslims changed their posture in the hope of regaining their lost prestige and power. The British took advantage of this situation and tried to wean away the Muslim leadership from the independence struggle by secretly promising them a separate nationhood. Thus began the chain of conflicts between the Hindus and Muslims. In the process, several Muslim organisations sprung up in the state. Some of the important ones are mentioned below:

Dar-ul-Uloom was established in 1867 in Deoband, Saharanpur district, by Mohammad Qasim Nanawati. The salient mottos of this institution were: trust in God, public co-operation, self-help, and democracy.

Sir Syed Ahmad Khan established in Aligarh in 1872 a Mohammedan Anglo-Oriental College based on the pattern of Ox-Bridge Colleges. This was later to become Aligarh Muslim University as a rival to Kashi Hindu Vishwavidyalaya in Varanasi. The main objective was to provide higher education to the Muslims so that they could compete for senior administrative positions in the government. Several writings on Sir Syed suggest that he helped the British during the 1857 revolt. He did everything to convey to the erstwhile rulers that the Muslims were dependent on them and were loyal to the British rule. Here is a sample of what he advocated:

> "When the naked 'truth' stands revealed with the glorious fact it stands out in prominent relief to the world that if in India there was one class of people above every other who from the principles of their religion, from habits and associations and from hundred dispositions were bound with Christians in their dead hour of trial and danger in the bonds of amity and friendship, then those people were the Muslims and they alone."[3]

Sir Syed took the view that both the British and the Muslims were in minority in India and that it was in their interest to work in unison to oppose the application of the

3. Syed Ahmad Khan, *An Account of the Loyal Mohammedans of India*, Meerut, 1860, Part I, p.3.

democratic principle. The anti-cow killing agitation by the Hindus gave an occasion to the leading Muslims to distance from the Congress---that was allegedly dominated by the Hindus---and forge a closer link with the British. The United Patriotic Association that was set up in the 1880s with the participation of both the Hindus and the Muslims, who expressed their loyalty to the Crown, got divided on the issue of the cow slaughter. The Muslim members regarded the agitation as anti-Islamic, and asked for the ouster of the Hindu members from the Association. In 1888, another effort was made to form a Mohammedan-Anglo Defence Association. In its founding meeting, Principal Theodore Beck went on to say that both the Congress and the agitation against cow slaughter were a combined attack against both the British and the Muslims. These efforts at creating associations by the Muslim leadership were blessed by the British who wanted to win over the Muslims from the Congress to weaken the freedom movement.

Following the setting up of the Aligarh Muslim University, another organisation by the name of *Nadwat-ul-Uloom* was set up in 1894 in Lucknow by orthodox Muslims. Its aim was to achieve a synthesis between *Dar-ul-Uloom* and Aligarh Muslim University. These have attracted Muslims from all parts of the country.

The Language Controversy

One of the key contentions between the Hindus and the Muslims in Uttar Pradesh was the use of vernacular language. It may be recalled that in 1837 the British replaced the Persian language as the official language by English. At that time, the vernacular language chosen for Uttar Pradesh, in addition to English, was Urdu in the Persian script and not Hindi in the *Devnagri* script. Urdu was thus made the official language for all administrative and judicial work.

As a reaction, the Hindus started demanding a place for Hindi language for official purposes. Finally, it was in response to Hindu demand that Hindi was accorded, in 1900, equal status vis-à-vis the Urdu language. Obviously, the Muslims did not like this; they strongly opposed the government order and organised anti-Hindi movements in the state. Even Sir Syed Ahmad Khan who founded Mohammadan Educational Conference opposed the demand for equating Hindi with Urdu. Muslims were so agitated over this issue that in 1928, in their representation to the Simon Commission, they demanded the abrogation of the 1900 order. They wanted Urdu to be the sole official and court language.

However, till 1920, Urdu remained a predominant vernacular language in Uttar Pradesh. Data on the number of Hindi-Urdu newspapers between 1873 and 1920 show the early dominance of Urdu language in the province.

Table 4

Number of Hindi-Urdu Newspapers, 1873-1970

Year	*Newspapers*	
	Hindi	*Urdu*
1873	9	25
1890	24	68
1900	34	69
1910	86	116
1920	175	151
1930	253	225
1940	367	268
1950	435	140
1960	594	161
1970	594	180

Source: Raghu Raj Gupta, *Hindu-Muslim Relations*, Ethnographic and Folk Culture Society, Lucknow, 1976, p.38

The Muslims were so determined and possessive to maintain their position that when in 1928, local self-government powers were extended to towns, they welcomed it because they were in majority in urban areas and were given weightage in political representation. But, when the same provisions were extended to the district boards, the Muslim leadership strongly opposed the move as in the rural areas they were in a minority, but used a different pretext. The Muslim leaders complained that, "District Board Act was hasty and a wrong Act. It conferred powers on an ignorant and illiterate peasantry and their power was, and has been utilised by members of the majority for the organisation and consolidation of their community and caste in the rural areas."[4]

After the 1937 elections, the Congress party got majority in the State Assembly and was able to form the government. This threatened the hegemony of Muslim elite class. They started demanding a separate homeland for themselves. The election results greatly shocked the Muslim leaders because the defeat signified considerable non-support even from among the Muslim voters. This naturally denied special powers to Muslims which they had hitherto enjoyed. As a consequence, they decided to demand a separate homeland for them. This is how began the movement for the creation of a Muslim independent state based on two-nation theory.

The Post-independence Phase

After the independence, the socio-economic and political profile of the Muslims in the state of Uttar Pradesh underwent a sea change, not because of any discrimination suffered by

4. Raghu Raj Gupta, *Hindu-Muslim Relations*, Ethnographic and Folk Culture Society, Lucknow, 1976, p. 42.

them but because several of the families of the Muslim elite, who were educated, modern and well-off, decided to migrate to Pakistan in the hope of better pastures; those who remained behind were mostly the rural illiterate craftsmen and poor farmers. As a result, their representation in government services, and their average per capita income, have fallen steeply. Thus, the population transfer created newer kind of imbalances, which reflected in the nature of Muslim participation in the economy. For example, current figures indicate that the percentage of Muslims in the Indian Administrative Service (IAS) is less than half of their percentage in the total population. Barely two per cent of government officers in senior positions, and less than half per cent of government clerks and peons come from the Muslim community. The same is true in the police force where the Muslims constitute only three per cent of the total police force. In the academe, the number of the Muslims is indeed very small. More distressing is the growth of *Dini Talim* schools. There are 6,000 such schools in Uttar Pradesh alone with an enrolment of six million students. These schools provide only religious education but do not prepare them for entry into the economy.[5]

Ignoring the reasons that changed the socio-demographic profile, the Muslim leadership attributes the degradation of their status to the biased policies of the so-called "Hindu dominated" government. And they make political capital out of it. The change in their status is the main reason of their anxiety and despair. The Urdu press has also contributed significantly to the aggravation of their discontentment.

Although, after 1920, the number of Hindi newspapers has

---

5. See, Asghar Ali Engineer, *Communal Riots in Post Independent India*, Sangam Books, Bombay, 1984, p. 212.

grown, it is important to mention that the number of Urdu newspapers, magazines, and weeklies has also increased tremendously after the partition and particularly during the 1980s---a fact that goes to contradict the general impression that Urdu was being throttled in the independent India, and especially in the state of Uttar Pradesh. The following table shows the comparative figures of Hindi-Urdu newspapers and other publications in the 1980s:

Table 5

*Hindi and Urdu Publications in Uttar Pradesh during 1980s**

Year	*Dailies*	*Weekly*	*Monthly*	*Annual*	*Total*
1980					
Hindi	136	1023	375	3	1537
Urdu	14	123	70	0	207
1981					
Hindi	NA	NA	NA	NA	
Urdu	NA	NA	NA	NA	
1982					
Hindi	151	1155	426	4	1736
Urdu	15	126	73	0	214
1983					
Hindi	156	1205	438	4	1803
Urdu	18	132	75	0	275
1984					
Hindi	173	1264	450	16	1903
Urdu	25	138	78	0	241
1985					
Hindi	195	1309	465	4	1973
Urdu	29	151	82	0	262
1987					
Hindi	248	1416	500	4	2168
Urdu	33	158	84	0	276

Contd...

Contd...

1988					
Hindi	257	1455	516	4	2250
Urdu	39	163	86	0	288
1989					
Hindi	285	1501	534	4	2324
Urdu	47	169	88	0	304
1990					
Hindi	314	1532	548	4	2398
Urdu	62	174	90	0	326
1991					
Hindi	269	1689	578	4	2520
Urdu	79	198	92	0	369

* *Press in India Annual Reports (1980-91)*, Registrar of Newspapers of India, Ministry of Information and Broadcasting, New Delhi.

After the partition the government abolished the communal electorate system; this adversely affected the Muslim elite of the state as they lost their exclusive constituency of Muslim following. On the other hand, the provision of joint electorate and institution of democratic politics enabled the various political parties to exploit the solid Muslim "Vote Bank". Muslim leadership also used this changed situation for its own political ends. But it is strange that the Muslim leadership never bothered to do anything about the economic and educational backwardness of Muslims.

In the 1980s the country witnessed the revival of Hindu militancy. The reasons for this revival were several, like conversion of Hindu Dalits into Islam in Meenakshipuram, self-assertion of Muslims, Khomeni's religious fervour in Iran, Zia's quest for Islamisation in Pakistan, Assam agitation and growing terrorism in Punjab. All these flared communal sentiments among the Hindus. Uttar Pradesh could not remain unaffected by these happenings.

In areas where Muslims have high concentration, they invite attraction of the political parties; the secular parties particularly try to woo them for their electoral support. Hindu-Muslim tensions and conflicts are the major social problems of the state. Frequent riots in several parts of the state have strained relationships between these two communities.

It will be useful to report here on some of the major communal clashes in the state of Uttar Pradesh.

Major Communal Riots in Uttar Pradesh during the 1980s

Communal riots are not new to the state of Uttar Pradesh. They are like an annual feature. The cities of Moradabad, Aligarh, Meerut, Allahabad and Azamgarh and some other districts are known to be prone to communal riots.

Before discussing the major communal riots that had occurred in Uttar Pradesh in the decade of the 1980s, it is pertinent to note the incidence of communal disturbances in the state from 1960 to 1980. The following table lists all the major riots in Uttar Pradesh in these two decades:

Table 6

Incidence of Communal Disturbances in Uttar Pradesh 1960-80

1968-69	*70-71*	*72-73*	*74-75*	*76-77*	*78-79*	*Total*
111	91	92	77	76	91	538

Note: Each column shows totals for two years.

Source: Home Ministry Reports.

In the decade of the 1980s major riots occurred in the cities of Moradabad (1980), Meerut (1982 and 1987), Aligarh (1985), Muzaffarnagar (1988) and Bijnor (1990). After 1986 the number of riots suddenly increased when a total of 244 riots occurred between 1986 and 1990 and almost all these had to do something with the Babri Masjid controversy.[6]

Below are described some of the communal riots that attracted nationwide attention.

Moradabad Riots-1980

Muslim population in Moradabad is 38.06 per cent of the total population. Refugee Punjabi families who settled down here after partition dominate brass business. This district has been the stronghold of the Congress. The former Bharatiya Jan Sangh---now called Bharatiya Janata Party (BJP)---also has strong supporters among the business class who have provided both political and financial assistance to the party. There is also evidence of growing influence of the Rashtriya Swayamsevak Sangh (RSS) in recent years. Beginning with 105 *Shakhas* (branches) with a membership of about 1,000, the number in 1990 has gone up to 170 *Shakhas* with a membership of over 2,500.[7]

Deliberate efforts have been made since 1971 to create rifts between the local Muslims and the Harijans (scheduled castes)---the two groups that have enjoyed favoured treatment from the Congress, and who have given it their unflinching support in the elections. Jan Sangh, however, failed in its attempts to create such a rift and ultimately the unity of Muslims and Harijans resulted in a smashing defeat of the BJP in the 1980 elections. This was a big setback for BJP. The Congress party succeeded in mobilising the Muslim vote bank despite the fact that a prominent Muslim League leader had extended his support to a BJP candidate. The fact that the Muslims had voted for the Congress was a disappointment for the Muslim League whose candidate had performed very poorly

6. Rasheeduddin Khan, op.cit., p. 224.

7. *Statesman*, New Delhi, 5 September 1980.

indicating that its strategy to communalise the elections did not bear fruit.[8] Following the election results, serious efforts were made by the BJP to woo the Harijans and bring them into the communal fold.[9]

On 13 August 1980, a major riot broke out in Moradabad which continued till November 1980. In this riot officially verified deaths---for which the government had paid compensation to the families of the victims—were 400. However, a Muslim group put the toll at 2,500. Other observers put the number between 1,500 and 2,000.

Here is the account of the riot based on the report published in *Sunday* (24 August 1980) by its Editor, M.J. Akbar:

On 13 August 1980, the day of Id, some 80,000 Muslims had gathered at the Idgah for the prayers. While they were offering *namaz*, a pig suddenly entered the mosque violating the sanctity of prayers. This infuriated the Muslims who thought that the Hindus engineered this sacrilegious act. They put blame on the Provincial Armed Constabulary officials who were posted there to guard the mosque and maintain law and order. Protesting for such an act of gross negligence, they asked the Provincial Armed Constabulary to remove the pig from the mosque compounds. But, the Provincial Armed Constabulary refused to remove it contending that it was not their job. This provoked the namazis who started brick batting. In the ensuing melee, the police officers were attacked, and the Assistant District Magistrate was even dragged off. The police retaliated by firing on the crowd that had assembled in the Idgah; this created a stampede causing death of several people.

While coming out of the mosque, the angry crowd attacked the nearby police post killing two policemen and setting ablaze

8. Krishna Gandhi, "Anatomy of Moradabad Riots", *Economic and Political Weekly*, 6 September 1980, pp. 1505-6.
9. *Patriot*, New Delhi, 27 August 1980.

the building. In retort, the Provincial Armed Constabulary brutally attacked the miscreants.

The police is said to have allowed students of K.G.K. College to attack Muslims of a nearby colony. These students also led a mob to Ramtalaiya village across the railway lines and burnt alive 15 men, women and children.[10] One of the several rumours was that the Shiva temple near the cremation ground was demolished and the priest killed by the Muslims. In retaliation, several Muslims living in *Line Par* areas were killed and a mosque was demolished. According to another rumour, on 14 August 1980, a Provincial Armed Constabulary (PAC) platoon was wiped out. Without verifying the veracity of this rumour, the infuriated PAC jawans killed ten persons who were in custody in the Kotwali.

In Patparsarai, a rumour was floated that Muslims were planning to attack the Hindus. This created panic and the Hindus got ready to fight them. Suddenly, a police jeep came and shot a Hindu boy dead. This event was explained by the police as an act of impersonation by the Muslim miscreants who came in police uniforms and killed the Hindu boy.

Initially curfew was enforced in Muslim localities alone. The police were reported to have made deals with the Hindu goondas over the sharing of loot from Muslim shops. It is reported that Hindus were also arrested but they were charged with light offence of breaking the curfew and were released on bail.

The then State Minister, Abdul Rehman Nashtar, openly accused the police for this turn of events. He said: "Although it was initially a clash between the namazis and the police, later on the police set some shops belonging to both communities on

10. Satish Saberwal and Mushirul Hasan, "Moradabad Riots, 1980: Causes and Meanings" cited in Asghar Ali Engineer (ed.), *Communal Riots in Post-Independent India*, p. 224.

fire to turn the attacks on the police into communal riot."[11]

Satish Saberwal and Mushirul Hasan write: "The magnitude of police violence had widespread repercussions in several towns of North India on 15th August. Moradabad police were under pressure to divert attention from itself. So it started inciting Hindus to attack the Muslims to simulate a communal riot."[12]

Raising the issue in the parliament, Shahabuddin, an MP, told that "Moradabad tragedy is like Jallianwala Bagh re-enacted. Both happened on the day of rejoicing. Both occurred in closed places. Firing in both the instances took place from the only exit and the point of entry that was there against the people congregated there". Comparing this incident with that of Jallianwala Bagh where the British police had killed freedom fighters was certainly an exaggeration, but it served to stir the Muslim community.

Seen objectively, this was not at all a case of riot between the Hindus and the Muslims; it began as a confrontation between the police and the Muslim congregation over mismanagement and negligence of duty. But it assumed a communal character, because the casualties on the police side were that of the Hindus, and on the side of the miscreants, of the Muslims. It is the status of the Hindu that was evoked rather than that of the police official. Such status displacement is quite a common phenomenon in situations of conflict. Since a comparison has been made with the Jallianwala Bagh, it may be said here in passing that in that event also the people who fired were the Indians serving the British government, although the orders were given by the British commanding officer. But

11. *New Age*, 24 August 1980.

12. Satish Saberwal and Mushirul Hasan, *"Moradabad Riots, 1980: Causes and Meanings"* cited in Asghar Ali Engineer (ed.), *Communal Riots in Post-Independent India*, p.223.

people's wrath was not directed against the Indians in the British service. In the Moradabad case, what started as a confrontation between the police and the Muslim devotees got generalised into a confrontation between the Hindus and the Muslims giving it a communal colour. It is alleged that the police made it look like communal to save its own skin. The former CPI MP from Amroha, Maulana Ishaq Sambhli and the Congress MLA from Moradabad, Hafiz Mohammad Siddiq, said in a joint statement issued on 14 August 1980: "The Moradabad disturbances are not communal in nature, but the administration is trying to turn it into a communal incident. If the police had not provoked the people by opening fire then these unfortunate developments would not have taken place."[13]

Analysts of the Moradabad case are of the opinion that the relative success and prosperity of Muslim businessmen in recent years was the main cause of communal problems in Moradabad. Muslim brassware traders received large orders from West Asia that gave an impetus to their trade and industry and attracted Muslim workers from the neighbouring districts. This generated hostility among the Hindu traders. This situation was exploited by the BJP which lost the 1980 election and was trying to regain the political dominance in the area. However, the immediate responsibility for the riots was placed on the PAC. The city police was alleged to have organised the beating, looting and killing of Muslims, provoked by the instigation that they managed to smuggle in the pig in the compounds of the mosque. The tragedy of Id day incident proved that the administration, the police, and above all the PAC at first disregarded intelligence reports of escalating group tensions in the district. They are also charged with grossly overreacting to the initial turmoil in the outer fringes of the Id congregation and finally of collaborating, whether by design or accidentally,

13. *New Age*, 24 August 1980.

with communal elements and goondas in fanning communal feelings between the Hindus and the Muslims.[14]

The RSS, on the other hand, put the blame on the then Union Home Secretary. According to *Organiser*: "It is of the view that Union Home Secretary, Syed Muzaffar Hussain Burney, had received advance intelligence of the threatened blow-up in Moradabad on Id day, but he neither informed the Home Minister, nor the Prime Minister, nor sent any CRPF or BSF reinforcement to strengthen the police presence in the mosque premises. It became clear that for maintaining law and order you do not need a Muslim Home Secretary but a competent Home Secretary."[15]

The officials and the press adopted a different line. They thought that it was the act of a foreign hand. Muslim educational institutions in Moradabad, receiving foreign money, were held responsible for engineering the riots. While addressing the Congress Parliamentary Board, Indira Gandhi also said: "The conflict was politically motivated and vested interests were attempting to undermine the peace and harmony in the country."[16]

Meerut Riots-1982

After Moradabad, Meerut became the second instance when the Provincial Armed Constabulary (PAC) was blamed, along with the local administration, for the riots. In both the cases, a minor issue was given the communal colour.

The PAC was alleged to have acted against the Muslims in the riots that occurred in Meerut in 1982. Reports said that

14. *Patriot*, New Delhi, 27 August 1980.

15. *Organiser*, New Delhi, 7 September 1980.

16. *The Times of India*, New Delhi, 21 August 1980.

between 29 September and 2 October 1982 police firing killed a number of people.[17] According to a Field Inquiry Report, the riots were well planned and lasted for more than four weeks. In these riots anti-social elements played a major role as they sought political legitimacy through participation in this communal conflict. They emerged as the saviours of their respective communities. Asghar Ali Engineer, who studied these riots in depth, was of the view that a conscious attempt was made to incite the *Dalits* to fight against the Muslims. According to him, it was rumoured that for killing a Muslim a *Dalit* was given Rs 200 and a bottle of liquor ![18]

Engineer traces its etiology to political rather than economic causes. Since Muslims in this constituency constitute a high percentage (49%), their support is considered very vital for any political party to win the election. Hence, all parties try to woo them and the Harijans.

However, the root cause of Meerut riots was a *Mazar-Mandir* (tomb-temple) controversy. In the commercial locality of Shahganj, there is a *Peepal* tree under which is located a shop of a beetle merchant and a water hut (*piao). Behind this *piao* is a well enclosed by high walls. Near this well there are three shops owned by a Trust. Adjacent to the well is a house of a Muslim advocate, Qazi Zaheeruddin. The dispute arose between the Trust and Qazi Zaheeruddin. The Hindus and the Muslims put counter-claims forward. The Hindus asserted that originally there was a temple under the tree; and the Muslims insisted that the place had a tomb of a Muslim saint. To assert their right, the Hindus started having evening prayers (*aarti)* with the playing of gong and conch shell. A *ghanta* (huge bell) was also installed there. As a result tension began to mount.

17. Asghar Ali Engineer, *Communal Riots in Post Independent India*, Sangam Books, Bombay.1984, p. 279.

18. Ibid., p. 274.

In April 1982, an enquiry was instituted. But, before the completion of this enquiry, the city president of BJP, Brahmapal Singh, and another BJP leader, Mohanlal Kapoor, performed *puja* at the site on 13 August 1982 and got arrested, only to be released at the intervention of the president of the local Congress. On 20 August 1982, an agreement was reached that neither the Hindus would ring the *ghanta,* nor the Muslims would press their claim for the use of the place as *mazar*. But, the Muslim leader (Hakim Saifuddin), who was not a party to this agreement, declared that he would spread a *chaddar* (a sheet of cloth) on the *mazar* as an offering. However, on 12 September 1982, the place was sealed by the authorities but the High Court held the attachment illegal. Thus, on 22 September 1982, the seal was removed. Next day, Mohanlal Kapoor led a victory procession in the town.

On the other side, on the Bakr-Id day (28 September 1982), the Muslims declared that they would demonstrate their protest by wearing black badges. They also hoisted black flags on their houses. Hindus reacted by hoisting saffron colour flags. The situation went out of control, and the police had to intervene. Between 30 September and 2 October 1982 several people got killed in the firing by the PAC. A delegation of prominent citizens came to the conclusion that all this had been done with careful planning and with the full participation of the PAC and the district administration.[19]

Meerut has been a Congress stronghold. Both the MLA and MP from this constituency belonged to this party. The BJP took advantage of this incident to break the Congress stronghold and make a dent into the Hindu vote. Therefore, it gave this minor issue the communal colour.

Similar riots occurred in Barabanki in 1986 and again in Meerut from 18 to 23 May 1987. In this second spate of riots, in

19. Ibid., p. 278.

Meerut district, a number of Muslims were killed in Hashimpura and Maliana. The government appointed a three-member Enquiry Committee presided over by Mr Gian Prakash to inquire into the Hashimpura and Maliana massacres. The committee said, in its report, that the riots were sparked by the decision to open the locks of the disputed Babri Masjid. According to this committee, the riots of April-May 1987 were pre-planned, organised and well-directed.[20] It also blamed the PAC for the killing of innocent people. Amnesty International also accused the PAC as a force modelled on the British military police of killing innocent Muslims in riots in Meerut.[21]

The General Secretary of the Indian Union Muslim League----C.M. Banatwala----submitted a memorandum to the President of India demanding dismissal of Uttar Pradesh government in the light of the report of Amnesty International on the Meerut riots.[22] Several Congress (I) MPs such as K.A. Abbasi, Zainul Basheer and Jaffer Sherief also held the PAC responsible for the killings in Meerut and asked the government to take disciplinary action against the offending police officials.

Fatehpur Riots-1987

The communal frenzy over the Babri Masjid dispute spread city after city in Uttar Pradesh. In July 1987, a communal tension arose in Fatehpur which had no history of communal tensions. It was around the time of Holi in 1986 that a small dispute over the location of a mosque and a temple in the town took a nasty turn and incidents of stone throwing were witnessed. However, the administration took effective steps to control it. But, in July 1987, the trouble started again when members of the Bajrang Dal chose to conduct an *Akhand Ramayan Paath* (uninterrupted

20. *Free Press Journal*, Bombay, 18 October 1987.

21. *The Times*, London, 20 November 1987.

22. *The Hindustan Times*, New Delhi, 1 December 1987.

recitation of the *Ramayana*) at a small temple built in a private house next to a mosque. The mosque authorities objected to use of a loudspeaker for the recitation of the *Ramayana*. At this, the administration tried to persuade the Bajrang Dal members to discontinue the *Paath* but to no avail. In retort, the leaders demanded the removal of the microphone and the loudspeakers from the mosque, which were regularly used to broadcast the *Azans*. Obviously, this was not acceptable to the Muslims. No compromise was thus reached and the tensions aggravated between the two groups.

The episode was, however, forgotten when a new dispute arose. The Arya Samaj began some construction on a piece of land that was used by the Muslims to keep the *Tazias* before being taken out for the Moharram procession. The Muslims objected to such a construction and asked for the maintenance of the *status quo*. The Administration stepped in and erected a wall there separating the two sites. Not approving this action, on 26 July 1987, the Muslim community observed strike by closing their shops as a mark of protest. This town that had inter-communal harmony hitherto thus became an arena of conflict. After this incident, the Muslims and the Hindus started holding two separate weekly bazaars, giving up the long tradition of a common weekly market. While no violent clashes occurred, the two communities became latently hostile to each other.

Aligarh and Muzaffarnagar Riots-1988

To protest against the long march to Ayodhya planned by the Babri Masjid Action Committee (BMAC) on 14 October 1988, the *Sri Ram Janma Bhoomi Sangharsh Samiti* called for a one-day Uttar Pradesh Bandh on 9 October 1988. The Bajrang Dal simultaneously announced that its members would go to the famous Jama Masjid in Delhi and recite loudly *Hanuman Chalisa* from there if the BMAC took out the march.

The entire Uttar Pradesh state observed the bandh on 9 October 1988. During this bandh, communal riots broke out in the towns of Aligarh, Khatauli and Muzaffarnagar that continued for full five days. The army had to be called in to quell the riots and the magistrate had to issue orders to shoot at sight. In these three towns a total of 15 persons were killed and 75 others were seriously injured. There were 21 instances of arson.[23]

Two of the Uttar Pradesh government ministers came under heavy criticism for their role in this episode. According to *The Telegraph*, the Minister of State for Home, Syeed Uzzaman, who hailed from the area, ordered the arrest of Shiv Sena workers, including its Meerut unit president Rajneesh Kumar Mittal. Two stage performers acting as Ram and Sita in *Ram Leela* show were also arrested. Subsequently, the supporters of another minister, Hukum Singh who also belonged to the area, held a meeting at Nainanadi Dharmshala on 10 October 1988, where he criticised Uzzaman severely and asked for his removal. The meeting was also addressed by Harish Chhabra, General Secretary of the Town Congress (I) and Dr Subhash Sharma of BJP. It was alleged that the supporters of Hukum Singh instigated the riots and even attacked the peace march near the Town Hall mainly to defame the Home Minister Uzzaman.[24]

Here, it is pertinent to mention that it was the Ayodhya movement which sought to give a new colour to the communal politics in Uttar Pradesh, specially after 1986. The outburst of communal tension in Meerut in 1987 and other cities of the state can largely be attributed to Ayodhya movement. Although communal riots were not new to Uttar Pradesh, the holocaust witnessed in the state after 1986 onwards superseded them all in its fury and intensity. More than 300 innocent lives

23. Ibid., 12 October 1988.

24. *The Telegraph*, Calcutta, 14 October 1988.

were lost in the course of a year, and half of them in Meerut alone. The Babri Masjid dispute adversely affected the cordiality of the Hindu-Muslim relations. The actual beneficiaries of this movement, which culminated into the demand for the construction of Ram Temple at Ayodhya, were the BJP and the VHP. It was basically the BJP that tried to exploit the religious sentiments of the Hindus in order to strengthen its political base in Uttar Pradesh. Since other issues had become redundant, the BJP raised the slogan of "Hindus in Danger". In fact, it was the 'Ram *lehar*' (Ram wave) that provided a new momentum to the consolidation of Hindu vote in favour of the BJP.

While the Ayodhya dispute precipitated matters, the communal tensions between the Hindus and the Muslims have a longer history. These were aggravated in the beginning of the 1980s when the country as a whole witnessed the resurgence of fundamentalism. Earlier, the riots were localised, caused by local factors and remained locally confined. But, in the decade of the 1980s, the riots originating at a place began to spread to other parts of the country, going beyond the borders of even a state. The Moradabad riots in 1980 were a turning point in the history of communal violence in Uttar Pradesh. The riots caused by the instance of a pig straying into a mosque in Moradabad spread as far as to Varanasi and Allahabad. The Muslims believed the allegation that the Hindus planned the pig entry into the mosque.

The Allahabad riots in 1980 also began over a minor quarrel between two youths of different communities over taking water from a public tap. The violence continued for a month. Similar was the pattern in Varanasi where riots broke out over the Durga Puja procession taking a particular route that passed through a street inhabited mostly by the Muslims.

But, the riots after the Babri Masjid issue defied all logic. However, the rift between the two communities started widening after the Supreme Court judgment in Shah Bano case in April 1985. Some Muslim leaders exploited the situation by hammering into the minds of innocent Muslim masses that the judgment was designed to be an attack on the Muslim Personal Law.[25]

The sustained mobilisation by the VHP for the liberation of Ramjanmabhoomi undeniably had given a new dimension to the Muslim protest against the Supreme Court judgment in regard to Shah Bano case (described in the last chapter). The government was in a fix. It had to appease both the Hindus and the Muslims. It therefore decided to enact the Muslim Women's Bill and at the same time to yield to the demand of the Hindus to open the locks of the Ram Temple. It was hoped that these two acts will divert the attention of the two communities from contending issues, and peace will return. But these hopes were shattered when the opening of the gates of the mosque resulted in thirty deaths due to violent clashes between the followers of the two faiths. The 1986 court verdict brought the long-standing dispute on the streets and subsequently to the political arena.

The Babri mosque issue continued to communalise the situation in Uttar Pradesh. We have seen as to how the communal politics took a turn at the hands of political parties over the issue of Shah Bano judgment and Ayodhya dispute. These two issues made the whole of Uttar Pradesh communally surcharged during the decade of the 1980s where serious riots broke out and a number of persons lost their lives. The Ayodhya dispute made the Congress lose the 1989 elections. Next chapter is devoted to the Babri Masjid controversy.

25. *Deccan Herald*, Bangalore, 20 September 1987.

5

The Case of Ayodhya

The controversy over Ramjanmabhoomi versus Babri Masjid is, no doubt, one of the most sensitive and emotional issues that polarised Hindus and Muslims in India. Different parties to the dispute played differently with the emotions of people on this issue. After February 1986, when the doors of the disputed shrine were opened for the Hindus to perform *puja*---to propitiate the deities enshrined there, on the orders of Faizabad court, emotions were aroused on both the sides. The Hindus felt elated as if they had won the long drawn-out battle for regaining their lost heritage; the Muslims, on the other side, considered it their defeat, as they were to lose control over a place of worship that they always claimed to have belonged to them. It was a zero-sum game: the loss of one party was a gain for the other. As it concerned the two major communities, the political parties jumped into the fray to exploit the situation for their political advantages. The secular among the Hindus wanted to keep politics out of this issue; but others interpreted this stance as a ploy to continue to get the popular Muslim support.

It is interesting to note here that in Indian politics, the distinction of the *secular* and *communal* is generally used only for the people belonging to the majority community. And, the word 'secular' is also narrowly defined as being sympathetic and supportive of the minority community, while professing oneself as a *Nastik* (agnostic, or non-practitioner of one's own religion). Given this popular perception, the media generally ignored the 'secular' among the Muslims and treated all of them as deeply religious and unanimous in their stand regarding the Ayodhya dispute. The Bharatiya Janata Party (BJP) was identified as the Hindu communal party compared to others that were regarded as secular. The All India Muslim League is regarded by some as a counterpart of the BJP. Just as not all Hindus belonged to the BJP, the Muslim League was also not joined by all the Muslims. Yet, there is one difference between them. Both in principle, and in reality, BJP's membership is open to the non-Hindus, it is not so in case of the Muslim League, as the name of the party itself suggests.

The 1989 and 1991 elections were fought on this particular plank and the consequence was that the Congress party, known for its secular stance and for its traditional support base among the Muslim voters, got badly defeated, particularly in the 1989 elections. The BJP, the right-wing party, was able to mobilise the Hindus on this sensitive issue. It succeeded in gaining more seats in the Lok Sabha and in various state assemblies throughout the country.

In order to better appreciate the issue, it is important to recount the history of the controversy.

The Babri Masjid: Origins

Mir Baqi, a noble of Emperor Babar's court, constructed Babri Masjid in 1528. On the walls of the mosque it is inscribed that the mosque was built on the order of Babar. Written in Persian, the inscription reads:

> By the command of Emperor Babar, whose justice is an edifice reaching up to the very height of the heaven; the good-hearted Mir Baqi built this alighting place of angels; Buwad Khair Baqi (may this goodness last forever) the year of building made clear likewise when I said, Buwad Khair Baqi (935 A.H.).

Another inscription on the outside of the gate reads as follows:

> In the name of one who is the wisest of all, who is the creator of the universe, but Himself has no abode; in thanks giving to the prophet of all prophets in the two worlds; in celebration of the glory of Babar Qualander (the recluse) who has achieved great success in the world.[1]

However, there is no mention in these inscriptions, as also in other chronicles of that time, to suggest that it was built by demolishing the Ram Temple. But it is popularly believed that Babar personally got it built after demolishing the Hindu temple. Subscribing to this, V.S. Naipaul wrote in his article published on 18 July 1993 in the *Times of India*: "In Ayodhya, the construction of a mosque on the spot regarded as sacred by the conquered population was meant as an insult." The VHP made loud claims that the Babri Masjid was located at *Ramjanmasthan* (birthplace of Lord Ram) where a temple existed from the time of King Vikramaditya.

"But another version of the Masjid's origins", to quote Harold Gould, "is that it grew out of a visit which Babar made to Ayodhya in 1528 to pay his respects to a famous *Fakir*, Quazal Abbas Qulandar, who resided there. In the words of Farzand Ahmed of Ayodhya: 'Fakir Quazal Abbas

1. K.N. Panikkar, "A Historical Overview", in S. Gopal (ed.), *Anatomy of Confrontation: The Babri Masjid and Ramjanambhoomi Issues*, Penguin Books India Ltd., New Delhi, 1991, pp. 27.

Qulandar...apparently asked Babar to demolish the temple and build a mosque where he could offer *namaz*. According to historical accounts, Babar was reluctant to do so, but the Fakir prevailed on him and his wish was carried out.'"[2]

Differences also exist as to whether this Ayodhya is the same Ayodhya as mentioned in Valmiki's *Ramayana* according to which Ram was born in the *Tretayuga*, thousands of years before the present-day *Kaliyuga*, sometime in 3102 B.C. The Ayodhya of *Ramayana's* description appears very different from the present day Ayodhya. Valmiki described that town as much developed with a luxurious material life. That description does not correspond with the archaeological evidence from the present-day Ayodhya. The excavations conducted in the area by A.K. Narayan and B.B. Lal suggest that habitation in Ayodhya began with the early phase of the Northern Black Polished Ware Culture. It means that the first occupation of Janmabhoomi area was in the 7th century B.C. Since there was no settlement in the region prior to this, it is argued by some historians that Ayodhya of Valmiki could not have existed at the present-day site.[3] They contend that literary, epigraphic and archaeological evidence from that period of Ayodhya does not collaborate the claim that there existed a Ram Temple, which was destroyed by Babar for building the mosque.

The dispute began in 1885 when the Mahant (head priest) Raghuvar Dass of the *Ramjanmasthan* filed a suit in the court of the Sub-Judge, Faizabad, on 15 January 1885, seeking permission to build a temple on the *chabootara* (platform) called the *Janmasthan*—an area of 17 feet by 21 feet situated on the outer enclosure of the disputed mosque to provide shelter for himself and other priests. In his suit, the Mahant said that in

2. Harold Gould, "The Babri Masjid and the secular contract" in Veena Das et al (eds.,) *Tradition, Pluralism and Identity*, Sage Publications, New Delhi, 1999, p.383.
3. K.N. Panikkar, Ibid., p.23.

May 1883, the Deputy Commissioner of Faizabad had refused permission to construct any temple there because of the objections raised by some Muslims. On 24 February 1885, the Sub-Judge, in his order, said that while the land on which the *chabootara* had stood belonged to the plaintiff and the property rests with him, he could not give permission to build the temple on the ground that it was too close to the existing mosque.

The Mahant then moved an appeal against this judgment to the District Judge. On 17 March 1886, the District Judge, Col. J.E.A. Chambier dismissed the appeal after an inspection of the site striking down the words from the earlier judgment which conceded that the property rested with the Mahant. The judge ruled that "a temple could not be built without inflaming communal passions. A railing was then built to separate the *chabutra*...from the Masjid. This imposed a physical boundary between Hindu and Muslim religious space ..."[4] Recording the judgment, the official made a very important statement: "I found the Masjid, built by Emperor Babur, stands on the border of the town of Ayodhya...It is most unfortunate that a Masjid should have been built on the land specially held sacred by the Hindus. But, as that occurred 356 years ago, it is too late now to remedy the grievance. All that can be done is to maintain the parties in status quo."[5]

The Mahant then moved to the Judicial Commissioner of Awadh seeking to quash the order of the District Judge. On 25 May 1886, the Mahant appeared before the Judicial Commissioner contending that the District Judge was wrong to cancel the earlier findings of the Sub-Judge and to state that Emperor Babar built the mosque. The Judicial Commissioner,

4. Harold Gould, op.cit., p.386.
5. As quoted by A.G. Noorani, "Legal Aspects to the Issue" in S. Gopal (ed.), op.cit., p.65.

W. Young, also dismissed the appeal on 1 November 1886 but observed that "this spot is situated within the precincts of the grounds surrounding the mosque erected some 350 years ago owing to the bigotry and tyranny of the Emperor who purposely chose this holy spot which according to Hindu legend was the site of the temple. The Hindus seemed to have very limited access to certain spots within the precincts adjoining the mosque and they have, from a series of years, been persistently trying to increase those rights and to erect buildings on two spots namely, Sita-ki-Rasoi and Ramchandra-ki Janmabhumi". He, however, said that the plaintiff's earlier suits had been dismissed on the grounds that the plaintiff had no evidence to support his claim that the land belonged to him.

This is how ended the first legal battle fought by the Hindus. The issue became alive once again in March 1934 when the slaughter of a cow in Shahjahanpur led to the communal riots during which the Hindus damaged its domes and demolished a part of the wall surrounding the mosque. However, with the intervention of the local administration further damage could be halted. The mosque was repaired by the funds collected through the fine imposed on the Hindu rioters.

In 1936, an enquiry was conducted by the then Commissioner of Waqfs regarding the history of the mosque. The Commissioner came to the conclusion that the mosque was built by Babar who was a Sunni Muslim. This report was made public in February 1944 through the official Waqf gazette.

There was another litigation concerning this mosque in 1945, but it involved the two sects of the Muslims---Shia and Sunni. Both the sects claimed the mosque. The 1945 litigation between the Shia Central Board of Waqf and Sunni Central Board of Waqf went to the court of the Civil Judge, Faizabad. On 23 March 1946, the Civil Judge, S.A. Ahsan, held that although the mosque was built by Babar who was a Sunni, there is evidence that the mosque was used by the members of both the sects of the Muslim.

A stir was created when on 22 December 1949 the Muslims discovered that the statues of Ram, Sita and Lakshman had been installed in the mosque. It later came to be known that this was done at the behest of two senior officials of the provincial government---the Deputy Commissioner (K.K. Nayar) and the City Magistrate (Guru Datta Singh), both having sympathies with the Rashtriya Swayamsevak Sangh.[6] Because of the involvement of the senior officials in the installation of the statues, the police picket on duty did not intervene in the matter. However, this incident was reported by the constable Mata Prasad at the police station next day. The police then informed the Chief Minister, Chief Secretary, Home Secretary and District Magistrate. When the news spread in the town, a large crowd congregated at the mosque to see the idols. The crowd gate crashed, breaking the doors; the police had hard time stopping the crowd and saving the mosque from further damage. It finally ejected the people out and sealed the gates. The police force at the mosque was reinforced. The District Magistrate refused to comply with the orders of the Chief Secretary to remove the idols saying that it would cause widespread rioting. A consensus was then reached to maintain the status quo till such time as the courts decided the ownership issue. And, the site was locked.

On 29 December 1949, the Additional City Magistrate of Faizabad and Ayodhya, Markendey Singh, appointed the Chairman of the Municipal Board of Faizabad-cum-Ayodhya, Priya Dutt Ram, as a receiver, to arrange for the care of the property in dispute. On 5 January 1950, the receiver took charge of the property.

---

6. See Harold Gould, op.cit., p.386.

On 16 January 1950, a civil suit was filed by Gopal Singh Visharad in the court of the Civil Judge, Faizabad praying to be entitled to worship and visit without obstruction the idols installed in the Janmabhoomi and seeking a perpetual injunction restraining the defendants from removing the idols. Among the defendants were five Muslims. The Civil Judge, M.M. Chadda, granted an interim injunction as asked for. The District Magistrate, Faizabad, instructed the district administration to move for modification of the order on the ground that the site in dispute was claimed by both the Hindus and the Muslims and that the public was not allowed to visit the shrine. And that if the Hindus were freely allowed for *puja* and *darshan* it would amount to only one party exercising its right.

The Vishwa Hindu Parishad[7] raised this issue during their *Ekatmata Yajna* and *Ekatmata Yatra* in 1983. But, this demand was very feeble and nobody took it seriously. But, in its first *Dharma Sansad* (religious congregation) organised on 7-8 April 1984 in Delhi, a *Ramjanmabhoomi Mukti Yajna Samiti* was formed with Mahant Avaidyanath as its president.[8] Under the aegis of this Samiti whose main aim was to "liberate Ramjanmabhoomi" several steps were taken for the liberation of the disputed shrine. One such step was *Ram-Janaki Rath Yatra* on 25 September 1984 from Sitamarhi (Bihar).

On 6 October 1984, on the banks of the river Sarayu, a large congregation took an oath for the liberation of the Janmabhoomi. A *padayatra* (a foot-walk) was undertaken from there to Lucknow with the demand for opening the gates (*Tala Kholo*) of the disputed shrine.

The *yatra* left from Lucknow on 16 October 1984 for Delhi to press its demands before the central government. But, due to the assassination of Indira Gandhi on 31 October 1984, the

7. Formed on 19 August 1964 with the aim of uniting and upliftment of Hindus.

8. *The Saga of Ayodhya*, Jagarama Prakashana Trust, Bangalore, 1990.

onward journey of the *yatra* was postponed. Again, on 26 March 1985, the VHP decided to recruit a suicide squad of five million people to liberate the Janmabhoomi. On 25 October 1985, the *Ram-Janaki Rath Yatra* was revived and a second *Dharma Sansad* was held at Udupi (Karnataka) to chalk out further action plans. The VHP threatened nationwide *satyagraha* if Ramjanmabhoomi was not restored to Hindus by 8 March 1986. On 18 December 1985, the VHP formed a Trust called the Ramjanmabhoomi Nyas. The Chief Minister of Uttar Pradesh, Vir Bahadur Singh, then met the VHP President Viswanath Katju to find a solution to the problem. But, there was no agreement, and on 16 January 1986, the VHP organised a *Sant Sammelan* (a conference of saints) in Ayodhya in which it was decided to start a struggle for the Janmabhoomi during the *Shivaratri* (last week of February).

Meanwhile, a lawyer from Ayodhya, Umesh Chander Pande, moved an application in the court of Sadar Munsif, Hari Shankar Dube, seeking an order to the respondents restraining them from imposing restrictions on *darshan* and *puja* offered by him and other members of the Hindu community. The Munsif turned down the request.

On 31 January 1986, the same lawyer then filed an appeal against this order before the District Judge, Faizabad. On 1 February 1986, the District Judge passed an order allowing the appeal and directing the respondents—who were the state of Uttar Pradesh, the District Magistrate, the City Magistrate and the Police Superintendent of Faizabad—to open the locks forthwith and not to impose any restrictions on *darshan* and *puja* of the applicant and other members of the community in general. The Judge in his verdict had said: "If the Hindus are offering prayers and worshipping the idols, though in a restricted way, for the last 35 years, the heavens are not going to fall if the locks of the gates O and P are removed."

Within 40 minutes of passing the order, the locks of the

main gates of the shrine were opened for the public. The event was telecast live.

Although the dispute had a long gestating period, it really picked up fire when the doors of the mosque were opened. The decision by the court created a sense of insecurity among the Muslims who began to feel that their identity was in danger. With the news spreading countrywide, tensions were heightened between the two communities. Muslims all over the country protested very strongly to the opening of the mosque for Hindus.

This initiated a process of confrontation and struggle with a view to protecting their threatened identity. In February 1986, the Babri Masjid Action Committee (BMAC) was formed with the sole purpose of mobilising the Muslims to protest against the reopening of the mosque for the Hindus. They struggled hard to get back the possession of the mosque. Reacting to this, the campaigners of Ramjanmabhoomi claimed that the question of the birthplace of Ram was a matter of faith that could not be settled through a legal process; the courts cannot ascertain it. But, the Muslims, on the other hand, wanted this dispute to be decided by the court. Both the parties remained adamant on their respective stands making this issue a matter of their prestige.

While the Hindu agitationists celebrated the opening of the gates of the disputed shrine, the irritated Muslims reacted adversely. As a response to the Muslim resentment, the Hindu enthusiasts began pressing for the reconstruction of a temple at this site. In retort, the Muslims began demanding the return of the mosque to them. While the VHP kept questioning the role of the judiciary in this case, the AIBMAC continued expressing its willingness to abide by the judgment of the court.

On 2 February 1986, a joint meeting of the Working Committee and the Central Action Committee of the All India

Muslim Personal Law Board was held in New Delhi to express "its deep sense of shock at the virtual handing over of the Babri Masjid in Ayodhya to the Hindu community without any decision on the substantive question of origin and title". It regarded this action as "complete travesty of justice and nothing short of legalised house-breaking". The meeting further observed: "This unilateral seizure will only serve to undermine the faith of the Muslim community in the political order and the judicial system."[9]

On 4 February 1986, Mohammad Hashim Ansari, President of the Babri Masjid Action Committee, moved an application for the stay of the order before the Lucknow Bench of the High Court. The Bench gave an order on the same day for the maintenance of the status quo till its further order.

Similarly, Muslim MLAs submitted a memorandum to the Chief Minister on 6 February 1986 demanding the following steps to be taken by the state government without further delay:[10]

1. Babri Masjid with all its appurtenant Waqf properties be protected and preserved in the form in which it existed on 22 December 1949 and its walls etc. be repaired and be kept intact.

2. Provocative slogans and speeches of the Vishwa Hindu Parishad and Bajrang Dal etc. be taken note of and immediate action be taken to stop the same and to punish the guilty persons.

3. Performance of *puja* and installation of idols inside the mosque or within its precincts be immediately stopped.

---

9. See *Muslim India*, Vol. IV, Number 39, March 1986, p.111.

10. Ibid., p. 200.

4. Muslims be allowed to offer prayers in the Babri mosque without any restriction and to manage the affairs of the same.

5. Possession of the mosque be restored to Muslims either by legislation or by getting the cases decided expeditiously.

To protest against the opening of the locks of the gates, the Acting President of the All India Muslim Majlis-e-Mushawarat, Syed Shahabuddin issued a statement on 6 February 1986 calling upon the Muslims to observe the day of 14 February 1986 as a "black day". In his letter to the Prime Minister, Shahabuddin wrote:

> The Babri Masjid episode in Ayodhya has created a deep sense of humiliation in the Muslim community. Dazed and frustrated, in their state of agony, they do not know what to do and to whom to turn…
>
> As a citizen, I feel that it will be a sad day if an entire community feels pushed against the wall with no one to speak for them and none to comprehend the anguish of their heart.

Shahabuddin asked the Prime Minister and the Home Minister for the intervention of the Centre in the matter, particularly to restore the status quo ante until the title suits are decided. He also informed the Home Minister about the decision of the Majlis-e-Mushawarat "to observe February 14 as day of mourning and prayer closing their establishments, hoisting black flags, and wearing black badges and submitting memorandum to the local authorities to demand the restoration of Babri Masjid to the community".

On 7 February 1986, the students of the Aligarh Muslim University met and passed the following resolution:

"The students of the Muslim University take the conversion of the Babri Masjid into a temple, after the recent writ petition against the Holy Quran in the Calcutta High Court, and the attack on the Muslim Personal Law in the Shah Bano case as a direct challenge to their self-respect and demand from the Government of India that situations should be corrected immediately so that the Muslim youth is not forced to adopt means which may prove disastrous for the country. We demand that in the Babri Masjid case the status quo ante should be restored.

We also demand that the doors of interference in the Muslim Personal Law should be closed for ever by deleting Article 44 of the Constitution."[11]

The Jamiat Ulema Hind Working Committee met in New Delhi on 21 and 22 February to discuss the issue of Babri Masjid and adopted the following resolution:

"The Working Committee of the Jamiat Ulema Hind expresses its serious concern at the Babri Masjid affair. This mosque has been a place of worship for Muslims for nearly 500 years. In the legal cases of 1885 and in official statements it has been recognised as a mosque. But in the tumultuous situation in 1949 it was locked due to a conspiracy. Since then the case is under hearing and despite High Courts instructions in 1955 for expeditious disposal, the decision has been deferred.

For nearly two years Vishwa Hindu Parishad and other organisations, which spread prejudice and hatred, began a campaign throughout the country to occupy the Babri Masjid by calling it Janamsthan of Ram Chandraji. Last month in a very objectionable manner, with the collusion of the administration, the Mosque was unlocked and Puja was permitted therein. The

11. Ibid., p.113.

Government also did not take any steps against this incredible injustice but assisted and encouraged it through radio and TV, nor was any ban imposed, on Rath Yatras and victory processions, which have led to riots and loss of life and property for the Muslims.

It is natural for the Muslims of India to feel restless and agonised. Muslims are tolerating their incalculable ruination but they are not prepared to tolerate the desecration of their places of worship. They are ready for the biggest sacrifice to defend them and when such an affair takes place with the conspiracy of the Government, the judiciary and the administration, the situation indeed becomes very grave. The Working Committee decides to convene a meeting of the *Mulk-o-Millat Bachao Tehrik* on 20th March 1986. to take appropriate decision for launching an effective movement. and demands the following:

1. Since the Government have admitted in the court in 1950-51 that the disputed premises is a mosque and is known as Babri Masjid and that Muslims have been offering Namaz therein for a long time and that this premises was never used as a temple of Ram Chandraji, the Government should re-state this position in clear terms that it recognises the premises, where Puja has now been permitted, as a mosque.

2. Because the order of the District Judge, Faizabad, of 1st February, 1986, is contrary to the stand of the Government, the Government of Uttar Pradesh should file a writ in the High Court against this order in order to have it nullified and appoint for the purpose lawyers who enjoy the confidence of the Muslims.

3. Effective steps should be taken to maintain the Babri Masjid and its attached properties in their original state.

4. The Government of Uttar Pradesh should appoint a Survey Team immediately to record, to photograph and to prepare

necessary plans of the present structure of the Babri Masjid and the buildings and properties attached thereto. This team should consist of two Muslims, two Hindus and a nominee of the court and submit its report within a week.

5. All pending cases relating to Babri Masjid should be decided within six months.

6. Until these cases are finally decided the status quo ante as on 31st January, 1986, should be restored.

7. Muslims should be permitted to offer Namaz in the mosque and its management should be handed over to the Muslims and the portions of the mosque, which have been damaged, should be immediately repaired.

This meeting appeals to the government and to the citizens to make every possible effort to maintain law and order and to restrain communal ill-feeling and expresses the hope that the Muslims will face this situation with patience despite provocations and act with wisdom and courage and in a dispassionate manner to counter the atmosphere of fear."[12]

On 24 February 1986, a Babri Masjid Action Committee was formed with the aim of getting the mosque back. Several Muslim MPs presented a memorandum to the then Prime Minister, Rajiv Gandhi on 3 March 1986, asking him to intervene to protect the interests of the minority community.[13]

Here is the text of the memorandum:

The recent judgement by the District Judge, Faizabad in respect of Babri Mosque, Ayodhya has caused deep anguish to the Muslim community and has created a grave situation in the country which, if

---

12. Ibid. p.114.

13. Ibid. p.115-116, and 126.

not tackled carefully can cause a national catastrophe beyond any cure. We, the Muslim Members of Parliament, therefore, desire to place facts before you and request you kindly to intervene in the matter urgently and restore confidence among the Muslim community that they should enjoy religious freedom as equal members of a secular state in accordance with the letter and spirit of the Constitution of India. At the very outset we assure you that the narration of the following facts is based on an overwhelming and irrefutable evidence in respect of the Babri Mosque's history and its legal position.

1. That, the Mosque was built during the regime of Mughal Emperor Babar by one of his Governors, namely, Mir Baqi on a vacant plot of land in the year 1528.

2. That, an internationally renowned historian A.S. Beveridge who has translated *Tuzuk-e-Babri* into English and given comprehensive footnotes, has in his book, *Memoirs of Babar* (Vol.II London, 1924, pp. 679-80) mentioned Babar's passing through Awadh. Beveridge has dealt with the subject with minute details but there is no mention of Babar having entered Ayodhya. After dealing with Sheikh Bayazid the rebel, who was Governor of Awadh, Babar appointed Baqui Beg Tashkandi (Mir Baqui) as Governor of Awadh and left. This fact is further proved by the report of District Commissioner of Waqfs, Faizabad, on 16 September 1938 submitted to the Chief Commissioner of Waqfs (U.P.). It is further more proved by the inscriptions on the walls of the mosque as acknowledged by the historian A.S. Beveridge and also by Pandit Hari Kishan the Sub-Judge, Faizabad in Suit No. 61/280 of 1885, vide his judgement dated 24.12.1885.

3. That from the above-mentioned report of District Commissioner of Waqfs, it is evident that two villages namely Bharaipur and Sholeypur were also granted as Revenue free land in the year 1864 for maintenance of the Mosque in lieu of the cash grant of Rs 60 per year originally sanctioned by Emperor Babar and subsequently enhanced by the King of Awadh to a sum of Rs 302.

4. That, in the year 1885 one Mahant Raghubar Dass had filed one suit in the court of Sub-Judge, Faizabad (Suit No. 61/280 of 1885)

and had alleged that the *chabootara* of Ram Janmasthan was without roof and building and the priests had to face great hardships on account of weather effects like excessive heat, cold or rain and as such, he prayed for permission to construct a temple over the said *chabootara* 21x17 ft. This suit was filed on 19.1.1885 and it was also contended in para 4 of the plaint that in April 1883 the Deputy Commissioner of Faizabad had refused the permission for construction of the said temple for reasons of communal harmony.

5. That, the Sub-Judge Faizabad, Pandit Hari Kishan dismissed the said suit No. 61/280 of 1885 by his order dated 24.12.1885. On the basis of the site plan prepared by the court's *Amin* one Mr Gopal Sahai, the Court observed that "in between the Mosque and '*chabootara*' there is a wall and it is clear that there are separate boundaries between the mosque and *chabootara* and this fact is also supported by the fact that there is boundary line built by the Government before the recent dispute". The Court further observed that "Around it there is the wall of the mosque and the word 'Allah' is inscribed on it and if permission is given to Hindus for construction of temple then one day or the other a criminal case will be started and thousands of people will be killed". And that "awarding permission to construct a temple at this juncture is to lay the foundation of riots and murders, hence the relief claimed should not be granted".

6. That, against the aforesaid judgement dated 24.12.1885 an Appeal was filed (Civil Appeal No. 27 of 1886—Mahant Raghubar Dass Vs Secretary of State and others) in the Court of District, Faizabad who ultimately dismissed it by his order dated 26.3.1886.

7. That, the Mosque was damaged in the communal riots of 1934 and the then U.P. government got it repaired.

8. In the 'Mis I band' Register of 1860 the said Mosque is recorded as Masjid Babari.

9. That, in the report of the Commissioner of Waqfs published in the Government Gazette dated 26.2.1944 this Mosque is mentioned to be a Sunni Waqf.

10. That, on the basis of the aforesaid facts the U.P. Sunni Central Board of Waqfs registered the said Mosque as a Waqf, namely, Waqf No. 26 of Faizabad under the U.P. Muslim Waqf Act, 1960.
11. That, up to 22.12.1949 regular prayers used to be offered by the Muslims in the said Mosque and it was in the night of 22/23.12.1949 that a violent mob of anti-Muslim fanatics forcibly occupied the Mosque with the connivance of the then District Magistrate Mr. K. K. Nayar who had to resign for his role in this sordid episode. And the idols of Sri Ram Chandraji were surreptitiously installed in the Mosque. The very F.I.R. lodged at Ayodhya police station by Constable Shri Mata Prasad posted at the site on 23.12.1949 corroborates the fact that idols were surreptitiously placed inside the mosque on the night of 22/23 December 1949.
12. That, on 23.12.1949 orders under Section 144 Cr. P.C. were imposed in Faizabad and Ayodhya and the Mosque was attached under Section 145 Cr. P.C.
13. That, on 16.1.1950 one Gopal Singh Visharad filed a suit No.2 of 1950 in the Court of Munsif Sadar, Faizabad. It is relevant to mention here the fact in the Court of Civil Judge, Faizabad that idols of Shri Ram Chandraji were mischievously put inside the mosque, has been admitted in the written statement dated 24.4.1950 filed by the Deputy Commissioner, Faizabad, J. N. Ugra in suit No.2 of 1950 as well as in the written statement of the state government in R.S. No.25 of 1950. Likewise another suit was filed by Nirmohi Akhara and ultimately a fourth suit was filed by the U.P. Sunni Central Board of Waqfs, Lucknow, in the court of Civil Judge, Faizabad, i.e., Reg. Suit No. 12 of 1961. All these four suits were consolidated and the Reg. Suit No. 12 of 1961 filed by Waqfs Board was made the leading case.

    From all the aforesaid written statements filed by State Government it is fully established that the State Government had all along been treating the said building as Babri Mosque and not as a temple of Sri Ram Chandraji.
14. In a matter relating to the receivership of the Mosque the file of the aforesaid leading case, i.e., Suit No.12 of 1961 was retained by

the Allahabad High Court and it is still lying in the same court (at Lucknow bench).

15. That, all of a sudden, on 25.1.1986 one Umesh Chander Pandey, an Advocate of Faizabad, moved an application in Reg. Suit No.2 of 1950 in the Court of Munsif, to the effect that D.M. and S.P. Faizabad be directed to remove the lock from the premises so that he and other members of the Hindu community may worship there. On 28.1.1986 the learned Munsif passed an order for putting up the application on the date fixed as the file of the case was before the High Court.

16. However, against the aforesaid order of Munsif, an appeal was filed before the District Judge on 30.1.1986, which was heard on 1.2.1986. On this date some Muslims came to know about these proceedings and moved an application for being impleaded as party to the appeal, as Umesh Chander Pandey had not impleaded any of the Muslim parties of the suits. The Muslims who were already parties in the original suits moved for implementation but all these prayers were unjustifiably rejected by the District Judge and he irrelevantly examined the District Magistrate and Superintendent of Police, who also seemed to have connived with the miscreants, and on the basis of their irrational and undemocratic statement that no law and order problem would be created if the lock of the mosque was opened, the District Judge allowed the appeal directing the D.M. and S.P. to remove the lock from the premises in dispute, and the lock was broken the same day at about 5.15 p.m.

17. That, it would be relevant to point out that the order, which has been obtained through conspiracy and without involving the Muslims, manifestly suffers from the following defects:

   (i) The applicant who has moved the application in question is not a party to any of the aforesaid suits and as such he has no *locus standi*;

   (ii) That, the Muslims who are parties in the aforesaid original suits and who also applied for impleadment in appeal, were not impleaded;

(iii) That the statements are never recorded in appeals as done by the erring District Judge;

(iv) The order passed by Munsif was not appealable as he had not yet decided the case;

(v) The appeal was heard by District Judge and one-sided orders were passed and implemented the same day;

(vi) And above all, no such order could have been passed when the record of the original is lying in the Allahabad High Court (Lucknow bench).

18. That, the order of the District Judge has resulted in the present situation—riots, imposition of curfew in many parts of the country, mass arrests. The order has caused a situation in which the confidence and faith of Muslims in the judicial system is shaken.

19. That, we feel constrained to charge that the National Television Network chose to be a party in the dispute by televising the entry of Hindu devotees into the Mosque and described the premises as 'Ram Janambhoomi'. All India Radio adopted the same attitude.

20. That, even the peaceful and democratic protest on the part of Muslim community was resented by the majority community with the active support of the law and order machinery.

21. What pains us most is the fact, that the values that could sustain and enrich a truly democratic and secular way of life in India are fast deteriorating and something needs to be done urgently if India has to remain strong and united. In this connection we would like to bring to the notice of the Hon'ble Prime Minister the full throated lament of Akshay Pandit, a freedom-fighter and a senior Congress leader of Faizabad, who had drawn the attention of Lal Bahadur Shastri, the then Home Minister of Uttar Pradesh in 1950, the high handedness and vandalism of some Hindu miscreants who wanted forcible conversion of Babri Mosque into a Temple.

Against this background, we, the Muslim Members of Parliament, request you kindly to take the appropriate measures to meet the following demands:

A. That you may kindly intervene in the matter immediately and take urgent measures to get the Babri Mosque restored to the Muslim community.

B. That, a writ petition be filed by the Government of U.P. in the High Court against the order dated 1.2.1986 passed by District Judge, Faizabad.

C. That as the District Judge himself has observed in his order dated 1.2.1986 that Authorities can independently take measures to maintain law and order, therefore, the status quo-ante as existed on 31.1.1986 should be restored in respect of Babri Mosque.

D. That all the pending suits relating to the premises in question be got disposed of within a period of six months.

E. That, a delegation of MPs representing various political parties be sent to Ayodhya to visit Babri Mosque and the same delegation be provided facilities to prepare a map on the premises as also to take photographs of the Mosque so as to bring on record actual existing position of the Mosque.

F. That the official media be directed not to describe the premises as Ram Janambhoomi.

This legal wrangle over the disputed shrine converted into a political battle between the BJP and the Congress. When BJP found Congress encroaching upon its Hindu vote bank in the beginning of 1980s, it encouraged. VHP to revive the Ayodhya issue. The VHP thus gave the clarion call "to liberate Lord Ram from his Muslim Jail"[14]. So powerful was the symbolism of this slogan that it adversely affected the Congress strategy to woo the Hindu voters, and the opening of the gates led many Muslims to part company with the Congress. The loss of the Congress became the gain for the BJP.

The Congress government at the Centre was clearly in a

14. Peter Van der Veer, "God must be liberated: A Hindu liberation movement in Ayodhya", *Modern Asian Studies*, Vol. 21, No.2, 1987, p.291.

dilemma. When it tried to pacify the Hindus by ordering the opening of the locks of the disputed shrine, Muslims got annoyed. When it tried to appease the Muslims by taking a sympathetic attitude towards the demand to protect the Muslim Personal Law, through enactment of the Muslim Women's Bill, conservative Hindus opposed the move and pleaded for a Uniform Civil Code. Appeasement tactic of the Congress did not work.

The Muslim organisations, having felt frustrated over the failure of their efforts to get the mosque restored to them, decided to boycott the Republic Day celebrations (26 January 1987), observe *Bharat Bandh* on 1 February 1987, and organise a protest rally on 30 March 1987. But, the decision to boycott the Republic Day celebrations was widely opposed and was branded as anti-national. In the face of mounting criticism, even from within the Muslim community, the boycott call was withdrawn.

The *Bharat Bandh* was, however, observed on 1 February 1987 with limited success. On that day a series of violent clashes occurred in various parts of Uttar Pradesh.

To counter the Muslims' move to plan a March to Delhi on 30 March 1987, the VHP organised 'U.P. Bandh' on 29 March 1987. Both the organisations started mobilising the masses on this issue. The Muslim rally at the Boat Club in New Delhi was rather huge; around three hundred thousand Muslims were said to have attended it. The Shahi Imam of Jama Masjid and many other leaders made provocative speeches at this rally. A Resolution adopted here was given to the Speaker of the Lok Sabha. It read:

> The rally regards the Babri Masjid as national heritage and as a historic monument but above all a place of Islamic worship whose sanctity must be universally respected by all right-minded persons whatever their religion. The violation of its divine

> sanctity should be regarded not only as an offence to the religious sentiments of the Muslims but also the secular order. The rally reiterated its determination and resolve of the Muslims of India to regain their Masjid however long and hard the struggle may be.

The success of the rally highlighted the growing resentment among the Muslims over the dispute and growth of new assertiveness among them. "The VHP responded to the 30th March rally of the Muslims by organising a mammoth rally of Hindus on 5 April 1987 on the bank of Sarayu river in Ayodhya and took a pledge to liberate the birthplace of Ram which was used as a mosque." The communal mobilisation by the conservative forces of both the communities resulted in terrible riots in Meerut, Modinagar, Muzaffarnagar, Hapur and Delhi causing deaths of hundreds of innocent people.

Encouraged by the success of Delhi rally, the Babri Masjid Movement Coordination Committee (BMMCC) ignored the *fatwa* issued by Dar-ul-Uloom of Deoband and decided to stage a march to Ayodhya on 14 October 1988 to offer *namaz* at Babri Masjid. To counter BMMCC's March, the Bajrang Dal announced to lead a procession to the Jama Masjid in Delhi for offering prayers to Hanuman.

The Union Government intervened at this stage to avert the crisis. It assured both the parties that it would soon activate the judicial process for speedy settlement of the Ayodhya dispute. On that assurance, the BMMCC called off the march to Ayodhya; so did the Bajrang Dal drop its plan to read *Hanuman Chalisa* at the Delhi Jama Masjid. The postponing of the march to Ayodhya caused split in the BMMCC in November 1988. The splinter groups renamed them as Babri Masjid Action Committee (BMAC) and the All India Babri Masjid Action Committee (AIBMAC).

Communal feelings were getting greatly intensified. Government talks with both the parties failed. The VHP and

Shiv Sena used every opportunity to aggravate the crisis. As the general elections drew nearer, the communalist elements in both the communities became more and more vocal and even violent. The VHP decided to hold a three-day conference in Allahabad from 27 through 29 January 1989, coinciding with the Kumbh Mela—the big religious congregation of the Hindus held every twelfth year at one of the four religious places by rotation. The Kumbh Mela congregation at Allahabad provided a veritable communal platform to the VHP, Bajrang Dal, and the RSS---the three major Hindu organisations that had spearheaded the Ayodhya agitation. These organisations did their very best to whip up communal passions among the Hindus. On the third day of the conference, a resolution was passed committing the conference to the cause of the liberation of Ramjanmabhoomi—the land where Lord Ram was born and which has been desecrated by the construction of a mosque on it. It was decided at the Allahabad conference that Hindus would defy the court verdict or any executive decision on the Babri Masjid dispute and would launch a campaign that would culminate in the laying of the foundation stone *(shilanyas)* for the Ram Temple on 9 November 1989. It was also decided to bring *Ramshilas* (consecrated bricks inscribed with the word 'Ram') from every village of India to the proposed temple site and to collect funds for the construction of the Ram Temple. The Allahabad conference was an eloquent demonstration of the capacity of VHP to effectively mobilise diverse sections of Hindu society for the religious cause of restoring the Ram Temple. The organisers of the conference said: "There are six lakh villages and 80 crore of Hindus in the country. If every village donated one brick and every Hindu donated just one rupee the battle for Ramjanmabhoomi would be half over." Accordingly, the VHP, the RSS, and Bajrang Dal started *Shila Pujan Samaroh* (brick worship ceremonies) from 30 September 1989 in six hundred thousand villages in India from where it was planned to take out the sanctified bricks in colourful processions to Ayodhya where they were to be laid in the foundations for the new Ram Temple.

To counter the efforts of the VHP and its allies for the massive mobilisation of Hindus across the country, the All India Babri Masjid Action Committee threatened to organise *hifazati dastas* (protection squads) to resist the approach of Hindu enthusiasts to the proposed temple site for the *Shila Pujan* programmes.[15]

The Bharatiya Janata Party decided, in its national executive meeting at Palampur (Himachal Pradesh), held in June 1989, to directly involve in the dispute taking the side of the VHP. In its resolution passed at this meeting, it said:

> The BJP holds that the nature of this controversy is such that it just cannot be sorted out by a court of law. The court of law cannot adjudicate as to whether Babar did actually invade Ayodhya, destroy a temple and build a mosque in its place. Even where a court does not pronounce on such facts it cannot suggest remedies to undo the vandalism of history.

It further called upon the Rajiv government:

> to adopt the same positive approach in respect of Ayodhya that the Nehru government did with regard to Somnath temple. The sentiments of the people must be respected and the Ramjanmabhoomi be handed over to Hindus if possible through a negotiated settlement or else by legislation.

Meanwhile, the Uttar Pradesh government decided to go to the High Court to grant an interim order. On 14 August 1989, the Court gave an interim order to maintain the status quo.

On the other side, AIBMAC and BMAC said that they would oppose any move to shift the mosque. According to

15. *The Times of India*, New Delhi, 4 August 1984.

them, "it is not the question of the structure of the mosque rather than the site on which the mosque stands that is more important".

On 27 September 1989, the Central and State Governments came to an agreement with VHP according to which the VHP assured to maintain peace and communal harmony. It was agreed that the VHP would abide by the High Court decision to maintain the status quo, and the government, in turn, would support and protect *Ramshila pujan* and the *shilanyas* scheduled for 9 November 1989. However, the processions provoked riots in several parts of the country. The BJP tried to consolidate the Hindu vote bank for the ninth general elections with this emotional issue and powerful and emotive slogans like:

> *Sougandh Ram ki khaate hai, hum mandir wahi banayenge* (We swear by Ram, we will build the temple at the same site).
>
> *Bachcha-bachcha Ram ka, Janambhoomi ke kaam ka* (Every child of Ram is for the birthplace of Ram).
>
> *Chahe panth anek hai, Hindu hum sab ek hai* (Despite different sects, all Hindus are one).

Despite all this, serious communal violence broke out in various parts of the country, especially in Uttar Pradesh, during the *Ramshila* processions.

On 6 November 1989, the State Government moved the High Court for seeking clarification whether the plot where the VHP planned to lay the foundation stone was disputed or not. The court in its order asked for the maintenance of the status quo and invited the State Government to clarify whether the plot which the Waqf Board had claimed as its property was disputed or not. Clarifying the point, the State Government said that plot (No.596) consisted of two parts, disputed and undisputed. The State Government was, however, told by the High Court that the site for foundation laying was a disputed one and that the August 1989 order to maintain a status quo was for the entire property that the Sunni Waqf Board had claimed, which included 23 plots adjoining the Babri Masjid. The Congress government took the view that the proposed site for the *shilanyas* ceremony was undisputed and therefore it allowed the ceremony to be performed.

The opposition parties regarded this action as part of the Congress tactics to garner Hindu votes. They alleged that the Congress government had the option of banning the *Ramshila* procession and of halting the *shilanyas* ceremony thereby forestalling so much communal violence but did not exercise it and let the Hindus perform the ceremony. The Muslims felt annoyed with the Congress for giving permission to the Hindus to perform the *shilanyas*. They regarded this as betrayal as it went against the promise given them.

The Muslims could not accept the Hindu move to build a temple on the site of the Babri Masjid. To stop the *shilanyas*, hundreds of Muslims courted arrest in Faizabad on the day chosen for the foundation laying ceremony. Since the Congress government allowed the performance of the foundation laying ceremony, the AIBMAC called upon all Muslims to withdraw support from the Congress in the forthcoming elections. The *shilanyas* ceremony contributed to the further deepening of the divide between the Hindus and the Muslims.

This Congress tactics of playing a double game---of trying to appease both the communities---did not succeed and the party lost miserably in the elections. The National Front (NF) government came to power at the Centre with the outside support of BJP and headed by V.P. Singh. In Uttar Pradesh, Socialist leader, Mulayum Singh Yadav, became the Chief Minister of the coalition government.

By mobilisation of Hindus on the Ram Temple issue, the BJP heightened its nation-wide visibility. The consecrating brick programme spread over three hundred thousand places in the country had succeeded in inflaming the communal passions of Hindus. According to the *Organiser:*

> The *shilanyas* issue and the BJP's stand that Janambhoomi should be handed over to Hindus and that the Muslim masses appreciate the strong Hindu sentiments on this issue and hand over the holy site to the Hindus obviously played a big role in the elections.[16]

The success achieved by RSS and VHP in the mobilisation for Ram Temple tempted the BJP to use the Ramjanmabhoomi issue for political gains. After the NF government took over, the VHP demanded early solution to the problem. And, since Vidhan Sabha elections were due in February 1990, they decided to start the construction of temple on 14 February 1990. The NF government pleaded with the VHP to give some more time to arrive at an acceptable solution to all the parties concerned. The VHP conceded this request and decided to postpone the construction work for four months. But nothing worthwhile happened. On 23 June 1990, at its meeting held at Hardwar, the VHP decided to start construction of the temple at Ayodhya from 30 October 1990. While supporting the NF government from the outside, the BJP also decided to join the VHP on this issue.

The NF government could not succeed in its efforts to find a suitable solution because both the parties—the VHP and the AIBMAC—were adamant on their respective stands. The VHP had already declared that it would not accept the judicial verdict as it was a matter of faith and belief. In a desperate bid to consolidate his position, the Prime Minister, V.P. Singh,

16. *Organiser*, 10 December 1989.

suddenly announced to implement the Mandal Commission Report on the Scheduled Castes and Scheduled Tribes. He took this measure mainly to consolidate his vote bank among OBCs and minorities. As was expected, this decision enraged the BJP leadership because the Mandal Report's recommendations went contrary to the interests of the upper caste Hindus. Opposing this move meant alienating the lower caste groups who had earlier been brought under the Hindu banner on the Ayodhya issue, and distancing them from the Muslims. While the upper caste Hindus supported the BJP in its opposition to the Mandal Report, and continued their demand for the construction of the Ram Temple, the lower castes viewed the BJP as the party of the upper caste Hindus who had continuously oppressed them as untouchables for centuries.

What the V.P. Singh government had intended had happened; the Hindus got divided, and the ruling party got hold of a vote bank that traditionally belonged to the Congress party. In one stroke, both Congress and BJP suffered losses at the hand of V.P. Singh. The BJP, therefore, reactivated its sentimental movement in the name of Ram to overshadow the Mandal movement and win back the support of lower castes. L.K. Advani, the president of BJP, decided to take over the leadership from the VHP for the Ram Temple movement and announced his 10,000 km long *Rath Yatra* (literally a voyage on chariot) from Somnath to Ayodhya to consolidate the Hindu vote. The *Rath Yatra* was proposed to start on 25 September 1990 from Somnath and culminate at Ayodhya on 30 October 1990. But Advani was stopped to complete his *yatra*; on 23 October 1990, the Bihar government arrested him at Samastipur.[17] Advani's technique of mass mobilisation and his brand of nationalism created fear psychosis among the Muslims. During his long *Rath Yatra*, provocative slogans were raised

17. *The Times of India*, New Delhi, 24 October 1990.

against the Muslims. A number of communal riots broke out in several parts of the country although not on the route taken by Advani for his *Rath Yatra*. Following the arrest of Advani that halted his *yatra*, the BJP withdrew its support from the NF government. Despite Advani's arrest, the leaders from the RSS, VHP, Bajrang Dal and Shiv Sena went ahead with their plan for the *kar seva* at Ayodhya on 30 October 1990. The Chief Minister of Uttar Pradesh, Mulayam Singh Yadav, was, however, determined not to allow the *kar seva*.

Despite multi-layered security arrangements made at the disputed site by the Mulayam Singh Yadav's government, *kar sevaks* managed to enter the mosque, damage its domes and hoist a saffron coloured flag on the top of the building. The security forces opened fire on the processionists forcing their entry into the mosque and killing a number of *kar sevaks*. This led to a new wave of communal riots. On 2 November 1990, the *kar sevaks* made yet another attempt to demolish the mosque in which, again, a number of *kar sevaks* were killed.[18]

As the news of symbolic conquest of the Babri Masjid by the VHP spread, the entire state of Uttar Pradesh was surcharged with emotion. The killing of a number of *kar sevaks* in this incident incited others partaking in *kar seva*. So as to avoid further clashes, the organisers decided to postpone the *kar seva*. To further their campaign, the VHP, and the RSS, decided to take the *asthi kalash* (urns containing ashes of the dead *kar sevaks*) to various parts of the country in a *Bhasmi Yatra*. This was yet another powerful symbol invented by the VHP for mobilising the Hindus and rallying them for a common cause.[19] These processions further ignited communal fury. A series of riots broke out wherever the processions carrying the *asthi kalash* were taken out. The first major riot broke out in Bijnor

---

18. Rasheeduddin Khan, *Bewildered India: Identity Pluralism Discord*, p. 247.
19. Ibid.

in Uttar Pradesh on 30 October 1990 where violence continued for full three days. The situation was quite explosive throughout Uttar Pradesh in the first week of November. On 1 November 1990 riots broke out at a number of places and curfew had to be clamped in 30 districts of the state.[20]

The *kar seva* on 30 October and 2 November 1990, and subsequent riots throughout Uttar Pradesh, attracted nationwide attention. In fact, this dispute became the main political plank during 1989-90. Both the BJP and VHP exploited Hindu sentiments to gain maximum political mileage. The reporting of these incidents by the local Hindi and Urdu press was so biased and provocative that it further aggravated the situation and deepened the communal divide. The Press Council expressed its deep displeasure and serious concern at the role of a section of the press, particularly of the multi-edition vernacular newspapers published from Uttar Pradesh, which commanded wide circulation. The Press Council issued an appeal to all the newspapers and newspersons "to strictly and faithfully adhere to and carry on the noble tradition of the Indian Press to maintain the highest standard of free, fair and objective journalism, particularly during the period of national crisis and communal and social strife."[21] To put an end to this, the Press Council of India set up a five-member committee to hear the complaints against the local press.[22]

Here it will be appropriate to mention some of the provocative headlines reported in Hindi newspapers. *Aaj*---published from Kanpur---gave very provocative headlines in its 3 November 1990 issue: *"Nihatte Ram bhakton ko gher kar*

---

20. Asghar Ali Engineer, *Lifting the Veil: Communal Violence and Communal Harmony in Contemporary India*, pp. 102-3.

21. Ibid., p. 116.

22. Ibid., p. iii.

ghanton firing----200 marey" (hours of firing on rounded up unarmed devotees of Ram---200 killed); *Kartik ke snaan par khoon se nahayee Ayodhya* (Ayodhya bathed in blood for its Kartika bath); *Jalianwala Bagh kand bauna pada* (the episode of Jalianwala appeared dwarfed). On 24 October 1990, this paper carried an item under the headline: *"Mirzapur jail mein Ram bhakton ko ghodey ki leed khilayee jarahi hai"* (the worshippers of Ram are being fed horse dung in Mirzapur jail).[23] The Agra edition of the same paper published an evening bulletin with the headline, *"Ayodhya mein firing, saikadon hatahat, sarkar dvara mritak sankhya panch batayee"* (firing in Ayodhya, hundreds injured, government figures say five dead). The Lucknow edition of 2 November 1990 of this Paper carried a headline, "*Sau se adhik lashen Sarayu mein phainki gayen*" (more than 100 dead bodies thrown into river Sarayu).[24] A special report carrying a list of missing persons released by the VHP was published with the headline, *"Yadi balidan nahin hua to kahan gaye ye 307 kar sevak?"* (if there were no sacrifices, then where did the 307 *kar sevaks* go?).[25]

A Lucknow daily titled, *Dainik Jagaran*, published in its special bulletin of 2 November 1990 that one hundred *kar sevaks* had died on the spot in indiscriminate police firing on *Rambhaktas*. The figure was reduced to thirty-two in the regular morning edition of 3 November 1990.[26] The same Paper, in its issue of 15 November 1990, wrote that Chief Minister Mulayam Singh was very angry that not enough bullets had been fired on the unarmed *Rambhakt kar sevaks* at Ayodhya during the *kar seva*. A subheading said that the police was not in favour of firing at the unarmed *kar sevaks,*[27] implying

23. Ibid., p. 113.

24. Ibid.

25. Ibid.

26. Ibid., p. 114.

27. Ibid.

thereby that the unwilling police force fired at the agitationists obeying the orders of the government.

The *Swatantra Bharat* of Lucknow reported the incident of 2 November 1990 with the headline, "*Nihatte kar sevaks ko bhoon dala. 100 tak ke marne ki aashanka, 25 lashen baramad, hazaron ghayal*" (unarmed *kar sevaks* massacred. Up to one hundred feared killed, 25 dead bodies recovered, thousands wounded).[28] Likewise, the *Swantra Chetna* of Gorakhpur, in its edition of 2 November 1990, published the news with the heading, "*Gorakhpurnath mandir ke gate par kabza, sadhuon mein dahshat, mandir ke pramukh dwar par virodhi jhande phahraye gaye*" (the gate of Gorakhnath temple seized, terror among sadhus, opponents' flag unfurled at the main gate of the temple).[29]

Opinions were divided on the issue of the Ram Temple. Mulayam Singh Yadav prominently displayed his pro-Muslim attitude. His speeches were very provocative which further communalised the already surcharged atmosphere. His state-wide *sadbhavana* (goodwill) rallies were conducted ostensibly to promote communal harmony, but the overriding message in his speeches was that the Muslims were under attack from the Hindus and that there was nothing wrong in their taking up arms in self-defence. He also never missed an opportunity to challenge the Hindu claim to build the temple on the disputed site. He firmly declared: *Masjid par ek parinda bhi par nahi maar sakta hai*---not even a bird can touch the mosque.[30] The impact of this assertion was electric. Even Hindus in rural areas, who were not so aware about the entire

28. Ibid.

29. Ibid., p. 115.

30. Smita Gupta and Vidya Subrahmanian, "Uttar Pradesh: A State Divided", in Asghar Ali Engineer (ed.), *Politics of Confrontation: The Babri Masjid-Ram Janmabhoomi Controversy Runs Riots,* Ajanta Publications, New Delhi, 1992, p.244.

controversy surrounding the Ram Temple, began to think that the government was going out of its way to appease the Muslims thereby hurting the Hindu cause, and even inflicting injury to their religion. The general feeling among the Hindus was that the Chief Minister was being partisan to one community. As things happened, it turned out that Mulayam Singh's secularism proved to be more harmful to the Muslims who had to pay a heavy price for it in subsequent riots that swept the entire state of Uttar Pradesh.[31]

The whole of Uttar Pradesh became a divided state. Even political parties were at a loss to decide as to whom to support. Many Hindus belonging to Congress and Janata Dal were also in favour of building the temple, if for no other reason than to net the considerable Hindu vote. Throughout the state, the VHP and Bajrang Dal workers indulged in provocative propaganda. They used the following slogans:[32]

> *Babar ki santan, jayegi kabristan*
> (The progeny of Babar will go the graveyard).
>
> *Saugandh Ram ki khaate hai, Mandir wahin banayenge*
> (We swear by the name of Ram that we will build the temple on that very site).
>
> *Tel lagao Dabar ka, nam mita do Babar ka*
> (Apply the oil of Dabar, and destroy the name of Babar).

The Chandra Shekhar government, which took over after the fall of the V.P. Singh government and with outside support from the Congress, tried to negotiate with both the parties for evolving a mutually acceptable solution. It asked both the

31. Asghar Ali Engineer, "Ram Janmabhoomi, *Kar Seva* and Communal Violence" in *Politics of Confrontation*, pp. 116-17.

32. Pradeep Nayak, op.cit., p. 150.

parties to give dependable evidence in support of their respective claims on the disputed land. But, the parties rejected each other's claims. Meanwhile, the VHP did another round of *kar seva* in December 1990 but it was of a low profile. This *kar seva* was intended to reiterate the intention to construct the Temple at Ayodhya. The leaders of the Temple movement were convinced that this would not be possible without changing the government both at the Centre and in the state. The VHP was convinced by the incident of 30 October 1990 that the symbol of Ram had the potential to garner Hindu votes and put the BJP into the saddle of power.[33]

Meanwhile, the Chandra Shekhar government had to resign as it lost majority support. The Lok Sabha was dissolved and the 10th general elections were announced. Both VHP and RSS held a joint rally in New Delhi on 4 April 1991 in support of the construction of Ram Temple scheduled for October 1991. Before that, a two-day *Dharma Sansad* was also held which asked the people to extend their cooperation in building the temple. The VHP asked the Hindu electorate to translate their Ram *bhakti* (devotion to Lord Ram) into votes for the BJP. For the 10th general elections, thus, the *Mandir* (Temple) and the *Masjid* (Mosque) became the main issue. The BJP promised the voters that it would create favourable climate for the construction of the Ram Temple if it were voted to power. The VHP, the RSS, and the Bajrang Dal busied themselves in mobilising mass support at the grassroots. They projected the elections as the fight between "Ram *bhakts*" (devotees of Ram) and "Ram *virodhis*" (the opponents of Ram). The Ayodhya dispute was characterised by them as an expression of *minoritism* and *pseudo-secularism* on the part of those who were opposing the construction of the Ram Temple while taking the side of the Muslims. The Hindu campaigners also showed video

33. *Ibid.*

cassettes of the police firing on the *kar sevaks*, which further provoked the Hindu sentiments. Their speeches were very communal in tone and content; they used the print media to carry their messages. See one such sample:

> You can run, but you can't hide yourself from the fact.
>
> This is not a new political struggle, it is the 77th attempt in the history to restore the Ram Janmabhoomi, our heritage.
>
> Thus far over 3 lakh *kar sevaks* had laid down their lives in the last 400 years.
>
> Pseudo-secularists wanted the mosque to be declared a national monument forgetting that Ram was an Indian and Babar an invader. It is a national dishonour if a symbol of invasion is so declared.
>
> Now ask yourself!
>
> Can even the most tolerant, most reasonable and peace loving Indian run away from his pride—the reason for his being ?
>
> The time has come to fight for our threatened faith.
>
> Hindus unite! Act as one.
>
> Not against anyone.
> But in defence of our motherland.[34]

The communal politics over the Ayodhya dispute played a determined role in the 10th general elections. It took a communal overtone. These elections proved that communal

34. *The Pioneer*, 11 May 1991.

politics had come of age as the main parties resorted to manipulating the religious sentiments of people. For the first time, in the political history of independent India, a religious dispute dominated the electoral scene. The Ayodhya controversy had been turned into a politics of vote banks to which all parties subscribed. The consequence was that no political party could get a clear majority at the Centre and the Congress party, for the first time, formed a minority government, headed by P.V. Narasimha Rao. In Uttar Pradesh, however, the BJP succeeded in forming a government.

On 7 October 1991, the BJP government of Uttar Pradesh acquired 2.77 acres of disputed land. The Chief Minister of Uttar Pradesh, Kalyan Singh, declared that the temple would be built as promised by the BJP. However, on 15 November 1991, the Supreme Court directed the Uttar Pradesh government to maintain the status quo at the acquired land till a court judgment was passed on the issue.[35] On the other hand, the Congress government at the Centre created a special Ayodhya Cell to deal with the dispute and tried to solve the problem through negotiations with all the concerned parties. The Prime Minister even declared in the Lok Sabha that the government would never allow the demolition of the Babri Masjid. The Lucknow Bench of the Allahabad High Court also warned the state government to restrain from any construction on the disputed site.[36] But, suddenly, on 30 October 1992, the VHP took a decision to hold another *kar seva* at the disputed site on 6 December 1992. The *Dharma Sansad*, held on 31 October 1992, attacked the Prime Minister for appeasement of Muslims at the cost of Hindu interest.[37] Ashok Singhal, President of the VHP, even warned the Prime Minister that if the Central

35. *Hindustan Times*, 16 November 1991.

36. *The Times of India*, 16 July 1992.

37. *The Pioneer*, 1 November 1992.

Government tried to stop the *kar seva* he would be ousted from Prime Ministership.[38]

Following this, the Central Government convened the meeting of the National Integration Council (NIC) on 23 November 1992. The NIC decided unanimously to authorise the Prime Minister to take whatever steps he deemed necessary to uphold the rule of law and the Constitution and to implement court orders on the Ayodhya dispute.[39] The NIC made the following suggestions:

1. dismiss the Uttar Pradesh government;
2. suspend the Uttar Pradesh State Assembly;
3. take over of the 2.77 acre of land acquired by the State Government;
4. protect the site with the posting of the central troops; and
5. refer the dispute to the Supreme Court.

The Congress was able to ensure that the Muslim leaders maintained a moderate and non-threatened posture. The Prime Minister told the Muslims: "I can fight the BJP but cannot, and no one else for that matter can, fight Lord Ram."[40] The implication of his statement was that the matter of temple was not confined to a political party but involved the sentiments of the entire Hindu community cutting across party lines.

The Muslims agreed to accept the verdict of the Supreme Court on Ayodhya and said that "they would give up their claim on the Babri Masjid if the Court held the view that it was built after demolishing the temple in 1528 A.D."[41] This was, however, not acceptable to the other party. The VHP leader

38. *The Hindustan Times*, 12 November 1992.

39. *The Times of India*, 24 November 1992.

40. *India Today*, 15 December 1992.

41. *Ibid.*

retorted: "The birthplace of Ram is a matter of faith and it cannot be determined in a court of law."

Nevertheless, the matter went to the Supreme Court. The Supreme Court asked the Uttar Pradesh government to report on the steps taken to ensure that the court injunction against the *kar seva* would be honoured. Since the arrangements for *kar seva* were already being made, Chief Minister Kalyan Singh pleaded for another week's time to negotiate and persuade the sadhus to abandon their plan. The apex court, however, gave him only three days' time and also hinted that it might ask the Central Government to appoint the receiver for the disputed land to ensure compliance with the court orders prohibiting construction of temple.

Sensing the imminent dismissal of its government in a swift last moment manoeuvre, the BJP made a tactical retreat. In the evening of 28 November 1992, the Supreme Court accepted a plea by the Uttar Pradesh government to allow the singing of hymns on the disputed site by *kar sevaks*. Moreover, it stipulated that a special judge would maintain scrutiny at the site and file daily report to the Supreme Court.[42]

India Today commented: "This was a notable climbdown from the fiery rhetoric of barely a week before when Kalyan Singh had pledged to sacrifice his government, and the VHP and the RSS leaders had made public announcement that during this round the battle would be decisive, that the *kar seva* would only stop after the completion of the temple."

However, despite the Uttar Pradesh government's assurance to the Supreme Court, BJP and its allies were determined "to erase once and for all the blot of Babar". The BJP began putting its alternative strategy together. But, the Congress failed to evolve its own plans to counter the BJP

42. Ibid.

strategy. The Central Government was informed by the Intelligence Bureau that the BJP, the RSS and the VHP were intending to demolish the structure. Ignoring the intelligence reports, the Prime Minister considered only the legal angle and was hopeful that the BJP will abide by the assurances it had given. But, the BJP pursued an alternative strategy taking advantage of loopholes in the orders of the Supreme Court. Despite the fears that already 15,000 *kar sevaks* had assembled and they were keen to defy the orders of the court, the Congress government went along with the BJP's legal assurance of a symbolic *kar seva*. This was a misjudgement, and the Congress had to pay a price for it.

The uncontrolled crowd that had assembled at the disputed site went berserk and demolished the mosque. This happened on 6 December 1992.

The whole country was shocked and surprised at receiving the news of the demolition of the mosque. It received widespread condemnation. Prime Minister P.V. Narasimha Rao said: "I have been betrayed by the BJP." He then held an emergency meeting of the cabinet after which President's rule was imposed in Uttar Pradesh with the dissolution of the State Assembly. The governments of three other states, where BJP was in power, were also dismissed. The Prime Minister also made repeated appeals for peace and communal amity on *Doordarshan* and the All India Radio. However, even before the dismissal orders were issued, the Chief Minister of Uttar Pradesh submitted his resignation. This he did within five and half hours of the demolition of the mosque when the situation went out of his control.

On 7 December 1992, the Supreme Court, during an emergency hearing on an application seeking the appointment of the Centre as a receiver of disputed property, said: "It is a great pity that a constitutionally elected government could not discharge its sensitive duties in a matter of this magnitude. This is the first time that an assurance by the state government that it will protect the structure and carry out the court orders has been violated." Expressing great concern over the repercussions of the demolition, the judges said that "innocent lives were being put to danger all over the country". K.K. Venugopal, the senior counsel for the State Government agreed with the judges and said that "the repercussions were mind-boggling for the future of the country. I hang my head in shame for what has happened."[43]

The senior BJP leader, Atal Behari Vajpayee, said that "the Ayodhya action was BJP's worst miscalculation and a misadventure."[44] L.K. Advani also said: "I am unhappy." And, the Chief Minister of Uttar Pradesh, Kalyan Singh, said that "I was kept in the dark." Whatever these BJP leaders said after the demolition, there was a general allegation that they were well prepared for this act and that they were making false promises to the Supreme Court, to the government, and even to the National Integration Council. After the 27 November 1992 pledge, RSS leader Rajendra Singh (Rajju Bhaiya) kept on assuring the Prime Minister that a negotiated settlement was still possible. On the other hand, M.M. Joshi was telling crowds, between December 1 and 5, during his own *yatra* to Ayodhya that "Muslims should not bother about a thousand bricks of a dilapidated structure as the Hindus had given them a whole country, Pakistan."[45] This statement made people believe that the BJP was all the time indulging in double talk. This impression is supported by what was said by a very vocal BJP leader, Uma Bharati: "It is the most blissful day of my entire life. I keep pinching myself to see if I am awake." The VHP's

43. *The Telegraph*, 7 December 1992.

44. *India Today*, 31 December 1992, p.53.

45. Ibid.

Ashok Singhal was unapologetic as he said: "Hindu sentiments in this country cannot be subjugated for long. This has been proved today." The Shiv Sena chief Bal Thackray proudly pronounced: "If those who stoned the disputed structure in Ayodhya were actually Shiv Sainiks, then I can only be proud of them."[46] When the Centre made the announcement that it will rebuild Babri Masjid, the BJP suddenly changed its stance and called for a *Bharat Bandh* on 10 December 1992 and warned that they will not allow anyone to rebuild the mosque at any cost.

After the demolition, the entire country witnessed a spate of violent communal riots in which around 1,100 people lost their lives. In Uttar Pradesh alone, 201 people were killed.[47] Muslims all over the country were very angry and outraged. They remained unconvinced by the measures announced by the government. The Shahi Imam of Jama Masjid said: "Muslims' faith and confidence in the government will not be restored till the idols are removed and reconstruction of the Masjid commences in Ayodhya."[48] The Naib Imam threatened that "Muslims in the country would not sit quiet and shall march to Ayodhya to reconstruct the Masjid themselves if the government failed to do so." He declared that Muslims still stake their claim to the disputed site. The Imam of Fatehpuri Masjid called for en masse resignation of all Muslim MPs and MLAs throughout the country in protest against the demolition.[49] By this act, the gulf between the two communities widened and the state was thrown on the defensive. H.D. Dua of *The Hindustan Times* said in his editorial "that the nation must hang its head in shame over what has happened in

46. Ibid.

47. *The Hindu*, 12 December 1992.

48. *Economic Times*, 10 December 1992, New Delhi.

49. *Pioneer*, 9 December 1992, New Delhi.

Ayodhya."[50] He implored his readers: "Don't bring politics into religion. It is difficult to delink them later on and don't arouse patience as it is difficult to tackle them later on."

The Ayodhya case influenced not only the politics in the state of Uttar Pradesh but the entire country. It added a new dimension to communalism. While previous riots involved the members of two communities on petty issues, the Ayodhya episode invoked the entire history of Hindu-Muslim relations. The issue was such that it earned support for the temple from all quarters of the Hindus, and for the mosque from all sections of the Muslims. It became the key talking point in all political rallies, and renewed the debate on secularism. Ayodhya has entered the political vocabulary of India. It has brought religion into politics and politics into religion.

50. *The Hindustan Times*, 7 December 1992, New Delhi.

6

Electoral Politics of Uttar Pradesh

Efficient functioning of electoral politics is crucial for the success of the parliamentary democratic system. Periodic elections provide the opportunities to the political parties to contend for political power. It is through this process that power changes hands; the people get an opportunity to exercise their right to punish or reward the political actors. Contending parties go to the public to enlist their support. It is the extent to which the parties are able to win over the confidence of the voters that determines their fate in the elections.

Despite deficiencies in literacy and economic advancement, the Indian electorate has shown its maturity by carefully exercising its voting right. India has seen changes of government through the ballot box. In the state of Uttar Pradesh also, governments have changed several times through this process. All this goes to prove that India is the only country in the South Asian region which has a functioning democracy for an uninterrupted period of more than five decades, ever since it attained its independence. It is true that under the changing compulsions of time and circumstances, political parties at times ignore normative considerations and resort to short-term gimmicks to wrest power but these do not challenge the democratic formula, and the electorate does not always oblige them. The power of the electorate has increased over time; it can no longer be taken for granted.

Broadly speaking, all the political parties profess to be secular in their ideology, approach, and orientation; the very character of the Indian population, which is pluralistic in terms of religion, language and sub-cultures, dictates this. However, political exigencies often obscure the normative ideal and the parties take recourse to non-secular tactics, making use of religion, caste, communalism, language and other regional factors in securing popular support. Whatever they find politically expedient, the political parties do not hesitate to make use of that factor. Since elections are based on the arithmetic of vote, political parties try to curry favour with the numerically preponderant primordial groups, be they caste, religion, ethnicity, or linguistic group. It is in this context that communalism is also brought into play in electoral politics of the country. The fact of the matter is that as India moves into the 21st century, caste and communal considerations are getting stronger in the political arena.

The agitation for the "liberation" of Ramjanmabhoomi at Ayodhya, which also resulted in the unstated consequence of dismantling of the mosque in 1992, should also be understood as part of the electoral politics. It is yet another glaring instance of the widespread communalisation of the Indian political process. The decade of 1980s was coloured by this dispute and affected political dynamics of the state as well as the country.

Uttar Pradesh occupies a commanding position in Indian politics. It has the largest number of the Members of Parliament (MPs); there are 85 seats from the state in the Lok Sabha. Its Legislative Assembly is also the biggest in the country having 425 seats.

In this chapter we will examine as to how the two prominent political parties, i.e., Congress (with an image of being secular) and the Bharatiya Janata Party (BJP—which is regarded as a Hindu party), have performed in this state and how Ayodhya controversy has affected the Lok Sabha and Vidhan Sabha elections during the 1980s.

BJP and Congress in the Indian Political Scene

Ever since 1967 when the country witnessed coalition governments in several states it was realised that in those constituencies where the Muslims were in large numbers, the outcome depended on the way they voted *en bloc.* Parties believed that the Muslims could swing the election results. This realisation has affected the party strategies and logistics. No party could afford to ignore such a large percentage of voters; each party adopted a strategy to win the favour of the Muslim voters. In this regard, Paul Brass has observed: "The belief that Muslims can be mobilised to vote *en bloc* for the party or a candidate perceived to be their protector leads to a competition for the Muslim vote which is often the largest or second largest potential voting bloc in Uttar Pradesh constituency. The heavy concentration of Muslim votes in several towns encourages competition among the various political parties for the mobilisation of the Muslim vote. However, Muslims and Scheduled Castes are considered to be the committed vote banks of the Congress Party. When this committed vote bank remains solid and the opposition is fragmented, a huge Congress landslide occurs, but when the opposition is united and major defections occur among the Muslims and the Scheduled Castes, then a big non-Congress victory is always likely."[1] Therefore, each political party tries to penetrate this

1. Paul Brass, *Caste, Faction and Party in Indian Politics, Vol. II: Election Studies,* Chanakya Publications, Delhi, 1985, p.13.

solid vote bank to change the balance of power. "In fact, ever since 1967, when signals had come from various corners that Muslims were not happy with the Congress it was realised that in a large number of constituencies their votes were more than just a force to reckon with, they could swing the results.... Courted in 1971, appeased in 1974, watched with amazement in 1977, Muslims in 1980 were sought after in the most blatant fashion. Discarded in 1984 they were to be wooed again in subsequent years."[2]

The performance of Congress and BJS/BJP in the Lok Sabha elections from 1952 to 1991 is shown below:

Table 1

Congress and BJS/BJP Seats in Lok Sabha in various Elections between 1952 and 1991

Year	*Congress*	*BJS/BJP*
1952	364(45.0%)	3(3.1%)
1957	371(47.8%)	4(5.9%)
1962	361(44.7%)	14(6.4%)
1967	283(40.0%)	35(9.4%)
1971	352(43.1%)	22(7.4%)
1977	154(34.5%)	295(41.3%)*
1980	353(42.7%)	31(19.0%)*
1984	415(48.1%)	2(7.4%)
1989	197(39.5%)	85(11.4%)
1991	231(37.5%)	119(19.9%)

*It was part of Janata Party.

Source: David Butler, Ashok Lahiri and Pranoy Roy, *India Decides: Elections 1952-1991*, Living Media India Ltd., New Delhi, 1991.

2. Violette Graf, "The Muslim Vote" in Subrota Mitra (ed.), *Electoral Politics in India: A Changing Landscape*, Segment Books, New Delhi, 1992, p. 213.

Seen in a nation-wide perspective, there is a distinct decline in the popularity of the Congress party as evidenced in the number of seats gained and percentage of votes polled in the Lok Sabha elections. Even in the first Lok Sabha elections, the Congress party received support from only 45 per cent of the electorate which came to an all-time low of 37.5 per cent in the 1991 elections—in fact, the situation has further worsened in the Lok Sabha elections of 1996, 1998, and 1999 where, like the 1991 elections, it lost not only the majority but also the polling percentage. Its best performance was in 1984 when it won 415 seats and 48.1 per cent of popular vote. In the 1989 elections, it got only 197 seats with 39.5 per cent votes. While in the 1991 elections, it improved its number of seats to 225---still lacking a clear majority---its polling percentage went down to 37.5. As against this, the Bharatiya Janata Party (BJP), in its earlier incarnation as Bharatiya Jana Sangh (BJS), began its account with just three seats and 3.1 per cent votes in the 1952 Lok Sabha elections, and reached an astounding figure of 295 seats (as part of the Janata Party coalition) with 41.3 percentage of the popular vote in 1977. In its own right, the BJP got 119 seats, with a popular vote of 21.9 per cent in the 1991 elections. In the elections of 1996, it further bettered its position by being the party with the largest number of seats (161 with 20.2% votes), although not yet gaining a majority. In subsequent elections, it won as many as 182 seats, replacing the Congress as the single largest party.

BJP and the Congress in Uttar Pradesh: An Overview

At the state level, in Uttar Pradesh, the BJP has been able to consolidate its position both in the Lok Sabha and the Vidhan Sabha. The performance of Congress and BJP in the state Lok Sabha elections from 1952 to 1991 can be seen from the following table:

Table 2
Congress and BJS/BJP Seats in Uttar Pradesh Lok Sabha between 1952 and 1991

Year	*Congress*	*BJS/BJP*
1952	81(53.0%)	0(7.3%)
1957	70(46.3%)	2(14.8%)
1962	62(38.2%)	7(17.6%)
1967	47(33.4%)	12(22.2%)
1971	73(48.6%)	4(12.3%)
1977	0(25.0%)	85(68.1%)*
1980	51(35.9%)	3(22.5%)*
1984	83(51.0%)	0(6.4%) BJP
1989	15(31.8%)	8(7.6%)
1991	5 (18.7%)	51(32.8%)

*It was part of Janata Party.

Source: David Butler, Ashok Lahiri and Pranoy Roy, *India Decides: Elections 1952-1991*, Living Media India Ltd., New Delhi, 1991.

In the Lok Sabha, while Congress came down from 81 seats in 1952 to five in 1991, the BJS/BJP climbed up from no seats in 1952 to 51 in 1991 and 52 in 1996. It is important to note that in 1977 elections, BJP and its coalition partners annexed all the 85 seats with the Congress drawing a blank for the first time. The Congress, however, improved its performance in the 1980 Lok Sabha elections because the Janata Party lost Muslim voters' support as they felt that it did not protect the cause of Urdu and did not take adequate steps to amend the Aligarh Muslim University Act. They were also annoyed that a Parsee, and not a Muslim, was appointed to head the new Minorities Commission. The increased incidence of Hindu-Muslim riots further alienated the Muslims from Janata Party. The frustrated Muslims went back to the Congress and voted for it in the 1980 elections.

Thus, the Congress won 51 Lok Sabha seats from Uttar

Pradesh in 1980 elections, with 35.9 per cent of votes whereas the Janata Party won only three seats with 22.5 per cent of votes. It is interesting to note that in the Ruhelkhand region, which has high incidence of Muslim population, Congress was able to win only five seats out of ten. This was a clear indication of the drifting Muslim vote although it did not go to the Janata Party cluster, which could not win any seat from this region. It was also the case in Upper Doab, which has sizable Muslim population. In this region,the Congress got only two seats out of 13, the rest went to "others". However, in the Poorvanchal region, the Congress performed better by winning 12 seats out of 19, whereas the Janata Party won only two seats with 26.3 per cent of votes. In Bundelkhand and Uttarakhand, the Congress won all the seats. In Awadh, it won 18 out of 21 seats, and in Lower Doab it got six seats out of 14, with only one seat going to Janata Dal.

From the state of Uttar Pradesh, 18 Muslim MPs were returned in 1980 elections. Of these, 11 belonged to the Congress.

A similar trend of the BJP incline and Congress decline can be seen in Vidhan Sabha elections in Uttar Pradesh. The performance of both the parties between 1952 and 1991 is given in the Table 3.

In Vidhan Sabha elections, starting from a mere two seats in 1952, the BJP had gone up to claim as many as 221 seats in the 1991 elections, but this figure came down to 174 in 1996 elections. As against this, the Congress has continually lost its hold, coming down from 390 in 1952 to 46 in 1991, and 33 in 1996.

As in the Lok Sabha elections, in 1980 Vidhan Sabha Assembly elections also the Congress was able to regain some of its lost territory because of the drift of the Muslim vote to its side. The Congress got 309 seats with 37.7 per cent of votes while Janata Party won only 11 seats with a meagre 10.38 per cent

Table 3

Congress and BJS/BJP Seats in Vidhan Sabha between 1952 and 1991

Year	*Congress*	*BJS/BJP*
1952	390 (47.9%)	2 (6.5%)
1957	286 (42.4)	17 (9.8)
1962	249 (32.2)	49 (16.5)
1967	199 (32.2)	98 (21.7)
1969	211 (33.7)	49 (17.9)
1974	215 (32.3)	61 (17.1)
1977	47 (31.9)	NA
1980	309 (37.7)	11 (10.8)
1985	269 (39.3)	16 (9.9)
1989	94 (27.9)	57 (11.6)
1991	46 (17.4)	221 (31.5)

Source: David Butler, Ashok Lahiri and Pranoy Roy, *India Decides: Elections 1952-1991*, Living Media India Ltd., New Delhi, 1991.

of votes. In this election, a total of 51 Muslims were elected as MLAs: 33 from the Congress, nine from Janata Party, four from Congress(U), one each from Lok Dal, CPI, and the Socialist Party, and two as independents. The Muslim candidates mostly won from those constituencies where the Muslim population constituted more than 10 per cent of the total.

While the Congress recovered some lost ground in the 1980 elections both for the Lok Sabha and the Vidhan Sabha, it suffered heavy losses in the subsequent Vidhan Sabha elections (held in 1983) in Andhra Pradesh and Karnataka---regarded as Congress bastions. This was also the time when problems occurred in the border states, and in the Punjab where minority communities took aggressive postures demanding greater autonomy and even seeking secession. This gave stimulus to the Hindu organisations to mobilise support. Threatened by such alarming tendencies and worried over the loss of support from the minority communities, the Congress was forced to search for a new electoral strategy. It began to talk about "threats to India's unity". This was to reassure the Hindus that the Congress party was equally worried about the growing trends and that it was not averse to the Hindu cause.

Capitalising on the growing communal sentiments of the Hindus, Indira Gandhi projected herself as the protector of the national interests. In one of her public meetings in Kurukshetra, Haryana, she openly attacked the minorities for creating problems in the Punjab and Assam. She said: "*Dharmayuddh* was underway to resist the challenge posed by the minorities." Following the Operation Blue Star of 1984 in Punjab, she said, in yet another meeting at Garhwal: "Hindu religion was under attack from the minorities." Such a stance won her widespread acclaim among the Hindus of North India.

After Indira Gandhi's assassination in October 1984, the Congress party chose her son, Rajiv Gandhi, as her political successor. He won landslide victory in the elections. He got the sympathy of majority of middle class Hindus throughout the country because they thought that his mother has sacrificed her life for a Hindu cause. He successfully projected the Congress party as the only one capable of maintaining the territorial integrity of the country. Such a posture by the Congress left the BJP, which had by then splintered from the Janata Party under the leadership of Atal Behari Vajpayee, in a dilemma. It could not oppose the Congress party on the stand it had taken against the secessionist demands of the Akali Dal; and it had no other pressing pretext to oppose the Congress. In 1984 Lok Sabha elections, the BJP could win only two seats with 9.4 per cent of votes drawing a complete blank from Uttar Pradesh. On the other hand, the Congress consolidated its position by securing 415 Lok Sabha seats with 48.1 per cent of votes; from Uttar Pradesh, it got 83 seats with 51 per cent of votes—an all-time high record for the party from this state. However, there were only 12 Muslims amongst the victors. Although the number of Muslim MPs was reduced from 18 to 12, the number of Congress Muslim MPs from Uttar Pradesh remained unchanged (11). However, only eight MPs were elected from the same constituencies as in 1980 elections three others won from other constituencies.

In all the regions of Uttar Pradesh the Congress party had astounding success winning almost all the seats. For the first time the party showed indifference to securing the Muslim vote. It was reported that the state Congress leaders openly criticised Muslims and lumped them together with the Sikhs as secessionists. Commenting on the election results, Brass wrote: "The 1984 elections showed that there existed a 'Hindu vote' which can be mobilised for the sake of national unity and threats from Sikh terrorism in Punjab and Muslim separatism in Jammu & Kashmir which could bring a landslide victory to a party."[3]

The performance of the Congress party at the 1984 Lok Sabha elections was repeated in the subsequent 1985 Vidhan Sabha elections in Uttar Pradesh. Exploiting the Hindu card, it was able to win a clear majority with 269 seats (63.3% of the total) securing 39.25 per cent of popular vote. Strangely, the BJP, which was identified with the Hindu cause, could get only 16 seats with 9.86 per cent of votes though improving both its number of seats and percentage of votes compared to its previous performance. However, the BJP drew a complete blank in Uttarakahand region, and could get only four seats in Rohelkhand and three in Poorvanchal whereas the Congress got 35 out of 50 seats in Rohelkhand, 69 out of 90 seats in Awadh (the locale of Ayodhya) and 54 out of 102 in Poorvanchal region.

3. Paul Brass, *The New Cambridge History of India: IV.1 Politics of India Since Independence*, Cambridge Press, 1990, pp.4-5.

In the 1985 Assembly elections 53 Muslim candidates were elected, out of whom 30 were from the Congress, 14 from Lok Dal, one from CPM, two from CPI, and three each from Congress (U) and independents. Thus, the number of Muslim MLAs increased only by two from the previous tally. At the same time, the number of Muslim MLAs winning on the Congress ticket declined from 32 to 30.

The Hindu card was so well played by the Congress that even the Rashtriya Swayamsevak Sangh (RSS) felt convinced to support it. Some key leaders of RSS so openly identified themselves with the Congress that they declared that they no longer considered the Congress as a threat to Indian democracy.[4]

Ayodhya and the Electoral Politics

The degrading defeat of the BJP in the 1984 Lok Sabha elections forced it to abandon its liberal and moderate posture and move to an aggressive and uncompromising stand on the issues of secularism and nationalism. As the Congress had already moved rightward after 1980, the BJP leadership felt that only by evoking the theme of majoritarianism and a confrontationist attitude towards the minorities would enable it to regain Hindu votes. Further, the Congress role in Shah Bano controversy and Ayodhya dispute made BJP fully convinced that Rajiv Gandhi government was bent upon playing the Hindu card in the next general elections as well. This was clearly perceived as a threat by BJP. A worried Atal Behari Vajpayee remarked: "We must not lose Hindu votes by letting him do that."

In the years following the elections, the politics was

4. It may be noted that in 1983, RSS workers had even worked for the Congress candidates in the Delhi local elections, which led to the Congress victory at the cost of BJP.

surcharged by two major issues, namely, the controversy created by the decision of the Supreme Court in Shah Bano case, and the growing demand by the Hindus to claim back the Ramjanmabhoomi in Ayodhya with an equally determined opposition by the Muslims with a view to protecting the historical Babri Masjid. The Vishwa Hindu Parishad launched a nation-wide movement to construct the Ram Temple at the site of the Babri mosque. A Ramjanmabhoomi Sangharsh Samiti was formed on 7 October 1984 to press the demand for allowing access to the Hindus to their religious site. This was strongly opposed by the Muslim leaders who formed the Babri Masjid Action Committee. Both these organisations launched counter-movements—one for the Ram Temple and the other for the protection of Babri Masjid. The Congress government had the difficult task of trying to appease both the communities.

The Ayodhya dispute became one of the most important factors for communal mobilisation by the BJP, the Congress and the Janata Dal in the 1989 elections. BJP grabbed this opportunity and tried its best to use these issues to consolidate the Hindu vote in its favour.

In the 9th general elections, held in the last week of November 1989, all the major political parties—BJP, Janata Dal and Congress---played the communal card. Due to the polarisation caused by the Ayodhya dispute, the BJP had no option but to concentrate on the Hindu vote; other parties, particularly the Congress, could not ignore the Hindu vote either; the Muslim vote alone was not enough for it to win. As it turned out, it was not the case of either-or for the secular parties. The voters were landed in a state of uncertainty.

In its anxiety to retain the Hindu support with it, the Congress party allowed the VHP to perform the *shilanyas* ceremony on 9 November 1989 notwithstanding objections from the Muslim organisations, such as the Babri Masjid Action

Committee and Muslim League. Muslims were very angry with this. As has been put by Vinod Mehta: "When future historians are pinpointing the day on which Rajiv Gandhi finally blew the elections they will most probably select the 9th November. On that day the Congress gifted away almost the entire Muslim vote in the country to the opposition---Janata Dal without making any fresh inroads into the Hindu vote to compensate for that loss."[5]

This pre-election communal mobilisation on the Ayodhya dispute by the Hindu and Muslim protagonists polarised the two communities. The VHP's 40-day long *Shila Puja* programme in half a million villages caused communal riots in several places in North India. The Ayodhya dispute, thus, became an important election issue. Different political parties responded to this controversy differently depending on their respective policy stances.

With the emergence of a powerful Hindu lobby and growing support for BJP and its allies, the Congress party could not afford to ignore the Hindus and depend solely on Muslims. Therefore, it adopted a policy of appeasement of both the groups as if it were carefully playing both Hindu and Muslim cards.

To woo the Muslims again, the Congress government in Uttar Pradesh introduced a legislation for granting Urdu the status of the second official language just before the elections, in September 1989. The BJP strongly objected to this move on the plea that it was motivated to gain Muslim support.

It was in this atmosphere that the 9th Lok Sabha elections and the Uttar Pradesh Vidhan Sabha elections were held. A feeling developed among the Muslims that the Congress had let them down; their leaders asked them not to vote for the Congress. Taking advantage of this, the Janata Party formed the

5. Vinod Mehta, 'Thank You and Good Bye', *Sunday*, 26 November 1989.

National Front with the left and regional parties and made seat adjustments with the BJP in order to defeat the Congress.

The National Front received the support of the Shahi Imam of Jama Masjid who issued a *fatwa* saying that the "Janata Dal had agreed to the conditions he put forward to lend his support and that V.P. Singh's stand on the Babri Masjid issues was fair."[6] In the 9th Lok Sabha elections Muslims voted *en block* for the Janata Dal. Several factors, including the support of the Shahi Imam and the issue of Bofors pay-offs, led to the defeat of the Congress. The Congress got 197 seats with 39.5 per cent of votes, BJP got 85 seats with 11.4 per cent of votes whereas the JP got 143 seats with 17.8 per cent of votes. The National Front formed its government with V.P. Singh as the Prime Minister.

In Uttar Pradesh, the scenario, by and large, was same: the Congress got 14 seats with 31.8 per cent of votes whereas BJP got eight seats with 7.6 per cent of votes and JP got 54 seats with 35.9 per cent of votes. The region-wise analysis of results shows that in this election, Congress was not able to get Muslim support. In the Muslim preponderant Rohelkhand region, it won only one seat and the BJP and Janata Dal together got eight seats. Similarly, in Upper Doab and the Awadh regions, which have high percentage of Muslim voters, the Congress was able to win only one and seven seats respectively out of a combined total of 34 seats.

It is important to note that only nine Muslim candidates got elected to Lok Sabha from Uttar Pradesh. Their number continued to fall from 18 in 1980 to 12 in 1984, and to nine in 1989. The most surprising was the fact that only one Muslim won on the Congress ticket, compared to 11 Muslim MPs elected on Congress ticket in previous (1980 and 1984) elections. Muslim candidates who had left the Congress before this election and joined Janata Dal, like Arif Mohammed Khan

6. Pradeep Nayak, op.cit., p.124.

and Mufti Mohammad Syeed, won this time on the Janata Dal ticket.

The election results showed that it was not only the Congress which failed to secure absolute majority in the Lok Sabha, no other party could claim a clear majority. But BJP's performance was the most significant feature of this election having won eight seats from this state. Congress party's stand on the *shilanyas* issue cost the party heavily in this election. The Muslims in northern and western parts alienated from the Congress for its failure to curb the riots and also for allowing *shilanyas* in the disputed area.

Similarly, in 1989 Vidhan Sabha election in the state the Ayodhya dispute dominated. As a result, the Congress could get only 94 seats with 27.9 per cent of the popular vote. The BJP got 57 seats with 11.6 per cent of votes. The main beneficiary was Janata Dal which got full support of the entire Muslim community thereby securing 204 seats.

The analysis of election results clearly reveals that in Rohelkhand region Janata Dal and BJP together got 30 seats out of 50. In the Poorvanchal region, they got 63 seats but in the Uttarakhand, the BJP drew a complete blank and the Janata Dal got two seats only. The Bahujan Samaj Party (BSP) was also able to win four seats from Rohelkhand region where it had an alliance with the Janata Dal. The role of the BSP in this election was significant as it eroded the Dalit base of the Congress party. The Congress, thus, lost its Muslim base to the Janata Dal, upper caste Hindu base to BJP, and Dalit base to BSP, virtually becoming a party without any vote bank.

Forty-one Muslim MLAs were elected to the State Assembly in the 1989 elections, this was twelve less than the previous election. The number of Muslim Congress MLAs also came down from 30 in 1985 to 11 in 1989. The Janata Dal got 13 Muslim MLAs elected on its ticket, whereas five won on the BSP ticket, two belonged to the CPI, one each to CPM and the

Lok Dal, and eight were independents. It is clear that Muslim support to Congress continued to decline as is evident from the number of Muslim MLAs winning on the Congress ticket—32 in 1980, 30 in 1984 and 11 in 1989.

After the National Front (NF) government took over at the Centre several rounds of talks were held to solve the temple issue but to no avail. The VHP remained determined to press this issue and continue to mobilise the people in its favour. On the other hand, the State Chief Minister also adopted the policy of maintaining the status quo. The atmosphere became very tense in the state. The key players in this game---VHP, RSS and the Bajrang Dal---aggressively continued their activities, mobilising the Hindus for the construction of the Ram Temple. While supporting the agitational politics of the VHP, the BJP also lent its support to the NF government at the Centre. The Hindu communal forces continued putting pressure on the Central Government of the National Front and the Janata Dal government in Uttar Pradesh to accede to its demand for building the Ram Temple at the birthplace of Lord Ram.

Unable to solve the Ayodhya issue, the Prime Minister—V.P. Singh—suddenly decided, on 7 August 1990, to implement the Mandal Commission Report on Scheduled Castes and Scheduled Tribes. The upper caste Hindus resented this announcement, resulting in the violent outbursts at several places. In Delhi, a student even immolated himself. The BJP saw in it an attempt by V.P. Singh to divide BJP's carefully consolidated Hindu vote bank. The Mandal Report served the function of creating a rift between the forward and backward castes. It was, indeed, a serious blow to the BJP, which was trying to consolidate its position among the Hindus. In his effort to repair the damage caused by the Mandal Report, the President of BJP, L.K. Advani, undertook a 10,000 km *Rath Yatra* from Somnath to Ayodhya covering ten states. Although there was no particular disturbance during his long journey with the participation of several thousand people all through his route, a series of communal riots broke out. Advani could not complete his *yatra* as he was arrested in Bihar. Following this, the BJP withdrew its support from the NF government, forcing the V.P. Singh government to resign. The Congress did not come to the rescue of the NF government either. Keen to enlist the Hindu votes in the next elections, the Congress supported the break-away group of Janata Dal led by Chandra Shekhar who succeeded in forming the government. The new Prime Minister, Chandra Shekhar, also tried in vain to solve this problem but did not succeed. Finally, the Congress withdrew its support from the new government and dissolution of the Lok Sabha, calling for fresh general elections.

The 10th general elections were held in a communally surcharged atmosphere. In this election, the main issue was Ram Temple at Ayodhya. BJP's main agenda for this election was: *Ram, Roti* and *Insaf* (Ram, bread and justice). It promised in its manifesto to bring about a *Ram Rajya*. In a meeting at Faizabad (the other name of Ayodhya), Atal Bihari Vajpayee declared that "Ayodhya dispute is not the simple question of constructing a temple or righting a historical wrong, rather it involves the larger question of reconstructing India's nationalism."[7] The meeting raised the provocative slogans such as: *kar sevako ka balidan, mang raha hai kamal nishan* (the sacrifice of the *kar sevaks* is asking for the support to the Lotus symbol); *Hindustan ne pukara hai, garam khoon hamara hai* (Hindustan is saying:the hot blood is ours). In order to counter Janata Dal's social justice plank which was to divide Hindu society on the caste lines BJP forged unity among various sections of Hindu society and started manoeuvring to persuade the backward sections of the Hindu society by raising the following slogans: *Jaat pant to chhood diya, Shri Ram se nata jod diya* (forgetting the distinctions of caste we have linked ourselves to Ram) *jan jan ki yahi pukaar; Ram bina jiwan bekar*

7. Pradeep Nayak, op. cit., p. 169.

(life has no meaning without Ram); *chahe pant anek hai, Hindu hum sub ek hai* (despite several sects, we all are Hindus).[8]

All other political parties in their manifestoes promised to maintain the status quo in regard to the Ayodhya dispute. The Congress, in its manifesto, said that the party was committed to finding a negotiated settlement of this issue which fully respects the sentiments of both the communities involved. It further said that if such a settlement cannot be reached, then all parties must respect the order of the court in this regard. The Congress, it must be said, was in favour of the construction of the temple at Ayodhya but was against the demolition of the mosque.

One can, thus, see that the main issue in the 10th general elections was secularism. However, due to the assassination of Rajiv Gandhi in 1991, in the midst of the election campaign, the BJP changed its election strategy by toning down its aggressive *Hindutva* campaign and advocating the need for "political stability". On the other hand, the Janata Dal fought this election in alliance with left parties to counter the threat posed by BJP's politics. On 3 May 1991, the Shahi Imam of Jama Masjid appealed to the Muslims for extending support to the Janata Dal.

In these elections, once again, the Congress failed to get an absolute majority. The BJP also did not get absolute majority despite its exploitation of the Ram Temple issue. Similarly, Janata Dal's appeal for social justice also did not work with the electorate. The Congress got 231 seats in the Lok Sabha with 37.57 per cent of votes. The BJP improved its position by securing 119 seats with 19.9 per cent of votes. The Janata Dal got only 55 seats with 10.8 per cent of votes. From Uttar Pradesh, the Congress got only five Lok Sabha seats while BJP secured 51 and Janata Dal 22 seats. Only three Muslim MPs were elected from state, out of whom two were from the Janata

8. Ibid., p.170.

Dal and one was from the Congress.

The number of Muslim MPs in the Lok Sabha fell from nine in 1989 to three in 1991. Realising that the Ayodhya dispute has created problems and that they may lose the support of the Hindu voters, many Muslim politicians decided to refrain from contesting, and to support those candidates who had a sympathetic attitude towards them. This probably explains the fall in the number of elected Muslim MPs from Uttar Pradesh. It is interesting that in the Ruhelkhand region the Congress drew a blank yielding seven seats to the BJP and three to the Janata Dal. The BJP also swept all the seats (eight) in the Bundelkhand and Uttarakhand regions. In Upper Doab and Awadh regions also the BJP got 67 per cent (8 and 14 seats respectively) whereas the Congress could not get a single seat in Upper Doab and only three seats out of a total of 21 in the Awadh region. The Congress similarly got one seat each in Lower Doab and in Poorvanchal compared to BJP's five and nine respectively.

By 1991, the religious-communal issues had become the predominant factors in Indian politics. That should explain the success of the BJP in winning over most of the Lok Sabha seats from Uttar Pradesh. This subsequently enabled the party to capture the major chunks of Vidhan Sabha seats as well. The Congress got 46 seats (17.4% of popular vote) while BJP got 221 seats (31.5% of popular vote).

Even though, neither the Congress nor the BJP was able to retain most of the seats from the Muslim dominated areas in the Vidhan Sabha elections, yet the *en bloc* voting of the Hindus for the BJP in view of the 'Ram syndrome' finally succeeded in catapulting the BJP into power in the state.

The decline of support to the Congress was visible in all the seven regions of the state. It secured only 10 seats out of 102 in Poorvanchal, four out of 50 in Ruhelkhand, two out of 68 in Upper Doab, and two out of 65 in Lower Doab, 21 out of 98 in Awadh, and three out of 14 in Uttarakhand.

In this Vidhan Sabha election, the number of Muslim MLAs fell to 23 from 41 in the previous election. Only four Muslims could win on the Congress ticket this time; 14 others belonged to the Janata Dal; two fought on the CPI ticket, one on the BSP, and two as independents. There is a clear trend of Muslim leaders drifting away from the Congress since 1980 as is evident from the fact that whereas there were 32 Muslim Congress MLAs in 1980 there number came down to only four in 1991.

Concluding Observations

To sum up, let us see the performance of the Congress and the BJP during the decade of the 1980s.

In Table 4 are given the percentages of votes polled in Uttar Pradesh, in its different regions, for the Lok Sabha elections, by the Congress and its main rival, BJP, for the four elections held in 1980, 1984, 1989 and 1991.

Table 4

Percentage of Votes Polled by the Congress and BJP in the last Four Lok Sabha Elections in Uttar Pradesh

Regions	*Parties*	*1980*	*1984*	*1989*	*1991*
Uttarakhand	Congress	52	62.6	38.5	33.4
	BJP	0	6.2	4.9	40.3
Ruhelkhand	Congress	32.9	45.9	27.0	19.6
	BJP	0	11.4	12.6	37.5
Upper Doab	Congress	31.6	51.8	35.2	17.8
	BJP	0	5	0.4	37.7
Awadh	Congress	42.9	56.8	33.6	20.5
	BJP	0	5.2	6.2	33.3
Lower Doab	Congress	31.1	49.5	31.1	15.8
	BJP	0	5.2	7.9	27.2
Bundelkhand	Congress	43.2	47.5	26.5	18.4
	BJP	0	10.7	22	31.9
Poorvanchal	Congress	33.4	46.9	26.4	16.2
	BJP	0	6.2	8.3	29.1

Uttarakhand

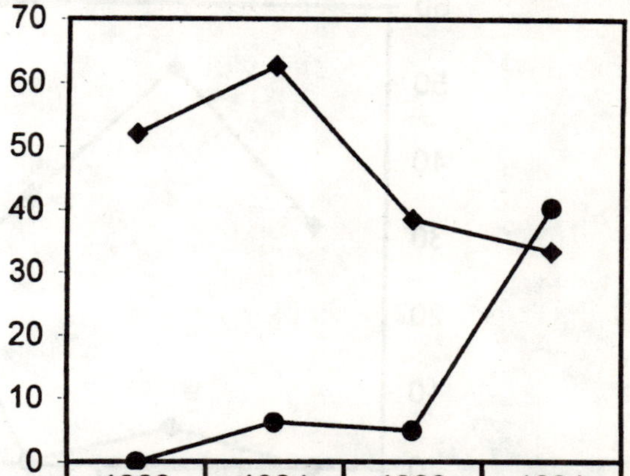

	1980	1984	1989	1991
Congress	52	62.6	38.5	33.4
BJP	0	6.2	4.9	40.3

Ruhelkhand

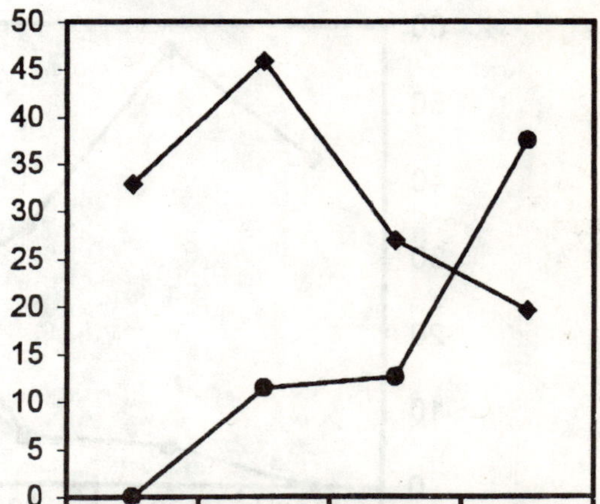

	1980	1984	1989	1991
Congress	32.9	45.9	27	19.6
BJP	0	11.4	12.6	37.5

Upper Doab

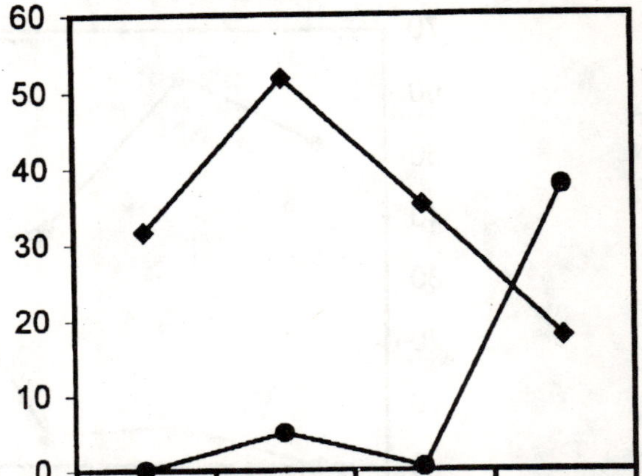

	1980	1984	1989	1991
Congress	31.6	51.8	35.2	17.8
BJP	0	5	0.4	37.7

Awadh

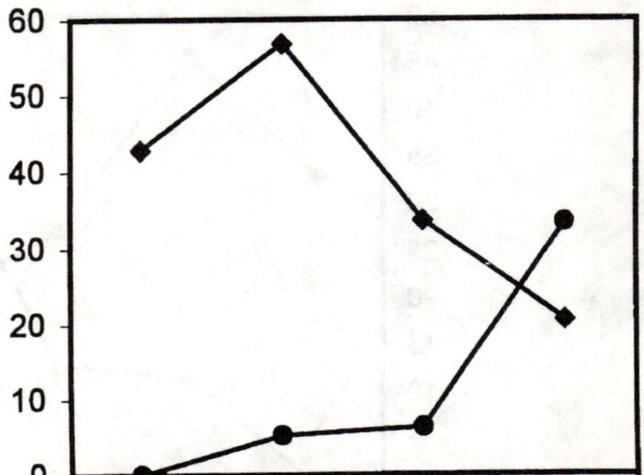

	1980	1984	1989	1991
Congress	42.9	56.8	33.6	20.5
BJP	0	5.2	6.2	33.3

Lower Doab

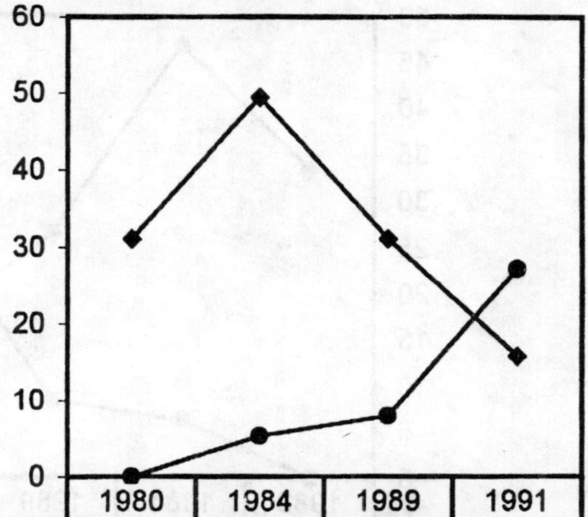

	1980	1984	1989	1991
Congress	31.1	49.5	31.1	15.8
BJP	0	5.2	7.9	27.2

Bundelkhand

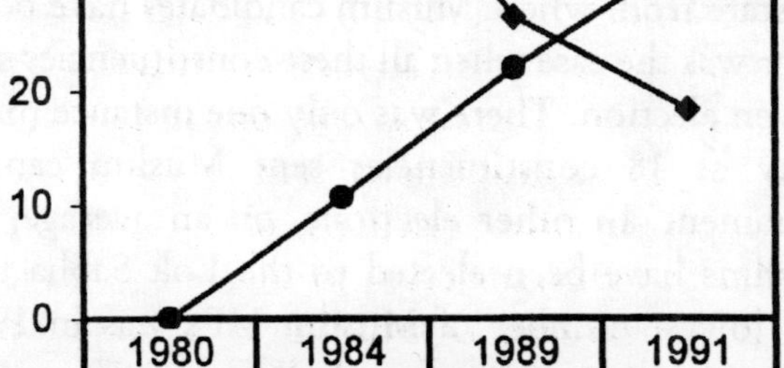

	1980	1984	1989	1991
Congress	43.2	47.5	26.5	18.4
BJP	0	10.7	22	31.9

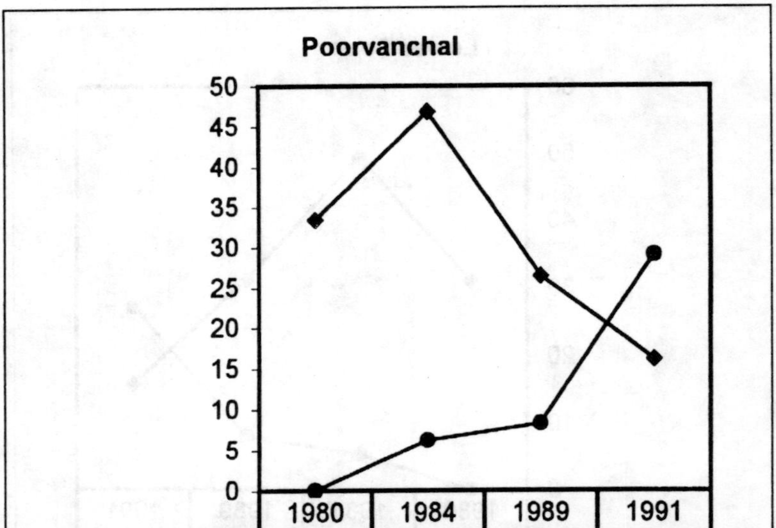

	1980	1984	1989	1991
Congress	33.4	46.9	26.4	16.2
BJP	0	6.2	8.3	29.1

The decline of Congress vote and simultaneous incline of the BJP vote can be graphically shown for each of the seven regions of the state.

Uttar Pradesh has always been sending some Muslim MPs to the Lok Sabha. An analysis of the first ten Lok Sabha elections, since 1952, suggests that there are 32 constituencies in the state from where Muslim candidates have been chosen. But never was the case when all these constituencies sent Muslims in a given election. There was only one instance (in 1980) when as many as 18 constituencies sent Muslim candidates to the parliament. In other elections, on an average, seven to eight Muslims have been elected to the Lok Sabha from this state. The lowest number of Muslim MPs was in 1991 when only three Muslims were elected. The constituency of Rampur, which has 47.95 per cent Muslim population, has the record of sending Muslim MPs for eight elections between 1952 and 1989 with a break in the 1977 elections; of these, seven had represented the Congress party. Moradabad has also elected Muslim MPs seven times, but only twice they represented the Congress. From Meerut, five times, the Muslims won and always on the Congress ticket. The constituencies of Baharaich, Mirzapur, Muzaffarnagar, Saharanpur, and Unnao sent Muslim MPs four times each. Bulandshahar and Kairana elected Muslims thrice for the Lok Sabha. The constituencies from where Muslim MPs were sent twice to the Lok Sabha are Badayun, Bareli, Bijnor, Chail, Domariyaganj, Etah, Farrukhabad, Fatehpur, Ghazipur, and Hapur. Twelve other constituencies, namely, Balrampur, Garhwal, Gonda, Hardoi, Jalesar, Jaunpur, Kanpur, Maharajganj, Pilibhit, Sambhal, Sultanpur and Tehri-Garhwal elected Muslim MPs only once.

It is interesting to note that no Muslim ever for once represented the Faizabad constituency---the locale of Babri Masjid and Ramjanmabhoomi. This constituency, which has 13.39 per cent Muslim population, had supported Congress candidates seven times; both Bharatiya Lok Dal and the CPI were each voted once in 1977 and 1989 respectively. The BJP got elected from here only in the 1990s—in 1991, 1996, and 1999 elections. In between, the Samajwadi Party got elected in 1998.

Here it may be interesting to compare the representation of Muslims in the Lok Sabha from Uttar Pradesh with the total of Muslim MPs in different Lok Sabhas.

The table suggests that Uttar Pradesh has contributed between 11 to 36 per cent of the Muslim MPs to the various Lok Sabhas. Their number was the highest in 1980 Lok Sabha when 18 out of 49 Muslim MPs were from this state. But then, their number began to decline returning to a meagre three in 1991---a position similar to 1957. It is also significant that while the Muslims constitute more than 10 per cent of the Indian population, their number in the parliament is between 4 and 9 per cent of the total seats in the Lok Sabha.

Table 5
Muslim MPs in Different Lok Sabhas (1952-1991)

Year	*Total Muslim MPs in LS*	*Muslim MPs from UP*	*Percentage of Muslim MPs*
1952	22	7	31.8
1957	23	3	13.04
1962	23	5	21.73
1967	29	5	17.24
1971	29	5	17.24
1977	34	9	26.47
1980	49	18	36.73
1984	45	12	26.66
1989	29	9	31.03
1991	27	3	11.11

There is no denying the fact that in the early 1980s religious issues did not dominate the electoral scene in Uttar Pradesh. At that time, the Congress party, by virtue of being the all-India national party, did not find any major obstacle in forming the government both at the state and central levels. But things changed owing to certain happenings in the country, such as the conversions to Islam in Meenakshipuram, and tensions in the border states of Punjab, Jammu & Kashmir and Assam. Reacting to the rise of such fundamentalism, political parties were willy-nilly drawn into the politics of religion. Even the so-called secular parties exploited the religious factor openly though they continued to project themselves as secular and criticised others for being communal and narrow minded. This change of strategy was clearly reflected in the electoral politics of the 1980s. The overall analysis of the assembly and parliamentary elections in the country, which took place in the later half of the 1980s, suggests that the religious-cum-communal issues largely governed the electoral politics. All the parties---be it Congress or the BJP or the Janata Dal---made effective use of religious-communal factors to gain political power and strengthen their electoral foothold. The state of Uttar Pradesh was no exception.

Perceiving a withering away of the Muslim votes from the Congress, the party ideologues started bringing about substantial changes and modifications in their electoral strategy for the subsequent parliamentary and assembly elections in Uttar Pradesh. The Congress realised the importance of the consolidation of Hindu votes for its long-term political strategy as it could now no longer think of relying on the votes of the minorities, particularly of the Muslims alone. Indira Gandhi took the initiative to project the Congress as a protector of Hindu interests. Rajiv Gandhi followed in her footsteps and even gave a religious colour to his mother's assassination. Hence, from 1984 onwards, the Congress was able to win over some more Hindu votes. The results also reflected that there was always a "Hindu vote in the making" which could be exploited for political dividends.

The religious approach adopted by the Congress made the BJP to rethink its own strategy so as to carve out a platform that would distinguish it from the Congress platform. The BJP found it electorally expedient to support the VHP movement for the construction of Ram Temple in Ayodhya. It took up a strong aggressive posture on abrogation of Article 370, Uniform Civil Code, and National Commission on Minorities, etc. It also started propagating *Hindutva* aggressively in the name of cultural nationalism. The Shah Bano controversy further helped strengthen the religious fervour of BJP's broad electoral strategy. These were the issues on which the Muslims differ and feel threatened. The other political parties taking the side of the Muslims and other minorities regarded the stand of the BJP as anti-secular and even anti-national.

From 1986 onwards, the Uttar Pradesh electoral politics took a turn. While the Muslims started getting alienated from the Congress and found in Janata Dal a possible alternative, the appeasement policy of the Congress, to assuage the Muslim feelings, cost them the Hindu vote, which went to the BJP. Although, in 1989 elections, the BJP could not form the government, because of its alliance with Janata Dal, yet the party substantially augmented its voting percentage and won more seats.

The developments from 1989 onwards further reflect the strengthening of the religious and communal fervour in the electoral politics of Uttar Pradesh. BJP had to dissociate itself from its alliance partner, Janata Dal, over the Mandal Commission controversy. As a result, the BJP pursued its agenda with a renewed zeal. Be it Advani's *Rath Yatra* or *Asthi Kalash Yatra* or Joshi's *Ekta Yatra*—all sought to strengthen the electoral base of the BJP in terms of forming governments in Uttar Pradesh, Madhya Pradesh, Rajasthan and Himachal Pradesh. But these actions contributed to the aggravation of communal tension in the country.

7

Concluding Observations

Prefatory Remarks

The decade of the 1980s witnessed communal disturbances in several parts of the country causing considerable unease and creating threats to the integration of the country. Let me recount the major communal clashes of the decade.

- The year 1980 saw display of intense communal sentiments in Moradabad when on the holy festival of Id, a pig entered a mosque disturbing the congregation offering Namaz. Hindus were accused for this sacrilegious act.
- In February 1981, as many as 143 families of the Dalits in Meenakshipuram in Tamilnadu were allegedly lured to conversion to Islam. This news was flashed throughout the country and gave rise to vociferous and even violent protests by the leading Hindu organizations, including the Vishwa Hindu Parishad. As a result, several of the 143 families so converted were reconverted by the Hindu enthusiasts with fanfare. To prevent recurrence of such conversions, the Vishwa Hindu Parishad organized a march

to emphasise *Ekatmata* (common identity) with a wide participation of Hindus from all walks of life. It culminated in Hardwar where a *yagna* (oblation to fire) was performed and a new temple dedicated to *Bharat Mata* (Mother India) was inaugurated.

In 1982, the city of Meerut became the scene for communal conflict when adherents of two faiths quarrelled over the boundaries of adjacent mosque and a temple.

The famous Shah Bano case relative to Muslim Personal Law became a matter of debate and discussion throughout the country in the year 1986.

In 1986, when on the one side Muslims were agitated over the possible attack on their Personal Law, the Hindu claim over Babri Masjid in Ayodhya as the birthplace of Ram intensified the tensions, on the other, the process of reclaim that begun in the previous year got further accelerated. The following years of the decade as well as the years of the next decade witnessed a spate of communal clashes in different parts of the country.

The demolition of the Babri Masjid in December 1992 ignited communal frenzy and involved the entire country in violent outbursts and in reprisals and retributions.

The decade of the 1980s thus saw communalism taking the central stage. Many characterised the emerging situation as *communalisation of politics* and *politicisation of communalism.* Originally employed, the term "communalism" had a positive referent, even a desirable trait of a community. But, in the Indian setting of a pluricultural society, "communalism" had always been used in the sense of a confrontation between two religious communities---a majority community and a minority community; and notwithstanding the presence of several minority religious groups, it was always referred to as a conflict between the Hindus and the Muslims. It is also important to mention that in this characterization, all the distinctions amongst the Hindus were conveniently ignored and people of different sects as well as Jains and the Sikhs were clubbed together.

The events of the 1980s changed the character of communalism. The earlier events were isolated happenings and were of a non-political character. But, in the 1980s, the political parties jumped into the fray and took advantage of the growing tension between the two communities to pursue their respective political agenda. It is this special feature that prompted me to investigate the new phenomenon. Since most of the events occurred in the state of Uttar Pradesh the book concentrates on that state.

Growth of Communalism in India

Although India was a subcontinent of various cultures---mostly autochthonous and indigenous prior to the arrival of so-called *Aryans* (espousing Vedic religion)---there existed harmony between different groups resulting into the formation of a Hindu civilisation. Interestingly, the Arab invaders coined the word "Hindu" much later for the people who were living along the Sindhu river. It is these invaders of non-Hindu origin, practitioners of Islam, who introduced a significant bipolarity in the Indian subcontinent, dividing the populace between Hindus and Muslims. All such invasions began with a confrontation, but later brought the warring groups---the outsiders and the insiders---closer through a process of accommodation and assimilation. These processes resulted in common sharing of several traits such as dress, language, food habits, mannerisms, and a common citizenry without erasing the distinctions of religion or sect or caste. It is this pattern of interactions that is held responsible for the formation of a composite culture of India.

The trend towards formation of a composite culture from

13th century onwards shows a number of enlightened rulers, sufis, writers, poets, artists and theologists belonging to Islam. In his book, *Bewildered India*, Rasheeduddin Khan has recounted contributions of these Muslim "pillars" of India's composite culture. "Baba Shaikh Farid (1173-1265), Nizamuddin Auliya (1238-1335), Nasiruddin Chiragh-e-Dilli (1296-1356) and Shaikh Abdul Qudddus Gangohi (1456-1538) were some of the sufi saints who immensely contributed to India's composite culture. Mention may also be made of Ziauddin Nakshahi (who translated 52 Sanskrit stories in his *Tutinama* in 1330), Qutban Jaunpuri (who wrote *Mrigavati* in 1501 in Awadhi language), Mallik Mohammad Jaisi (1493-1542) (whose poetry books of *Padmavat* and *Akhrawat* established a new trend in Hindi language and literature). Similarly, Hammad compiled the first book in Persian on Indian music called *Lahzat-e-Sikandari* in Sikandar Lodhi's time. Shah Manjhan Jaunpuri composed *Madhumalti* (1545) during the reign of Akbar. Sheikh Nabi Naunpuri's *Jnan Deep* was written in Jahangir's reign. Sultan Ibrahim Adil Shah's pioneering book on Indian music called *Kitab-e-Nauras* (1600), Mullah Nusrati of Bijapur's *Manohar* and *Madhumati* (1657), Ishrati's *Deepak Patan*, and *Chaatlagan* in the same style as Mallik Mohammad Jaisi's, Muquini's *Chandarbhan wa Mahyar* (1657), Mullah Wajhi's *Qutub-mushtani* (1610) in Dakhini Urdu, Faizi's (1547-95) translation of *Mahabharat* and of *Nal* and *Damayanti* into Persian language, Abdul Rahim Khan-e-Khanan's (1556-1627) poetry especially his *Nayika Bheda* in *Barve* meter, Raskhan's *Sajjan Raskhan* and *Prem Vatika* and Mohammad's *Indrawati* (1744), are some examples of elegant poetry by Muslim litterateurs of that glorious period. The well-known personalities like Shaukat Ali Khan Fani, Asghaar Hussain Asghar Gondvi, Ali Sikander, Jigar Moradabadi, and several others are shining examples of our composite culture in modern times". These Muslims who contributed to India's heritage have done so, says Rasheeduddin Khan, "as Indians by fully identifying themselves with the Indian nation."[1]

Even in the recent times, examples of Muslims contributing to the composite culture of India are in abundance. Bade Gulam Ali Khan's rendering of the Hindu devotional song *Hari Om Tatsat* is appreciated even today. When the country was divided over the issue of Ram Mandir versus Babri Masjid, it was a Muslim writer, Rahi Masoom Raza, who wrote the script and dialogues of the famous TV serial on the great Hindu epic, *Mahabharata*. Most of the Hindu devotional songs in Hindi films were sung by Muslim singers such as Mohammad Rafi and composed by Naushad Ali. One needs only remind oneself of the number of times Muslim actors have played the roles of Hindu devotees in Hindi films, and have been shown entering the temples, and never has any Hindu objected to this in the name of defiling the 'holy premises'.

The fact that there is a long and disturbing history of communal clashes goes to negate the claims of a composite culture. There are zealots, both among the Muslims and the Hindus, who deny the existence of such a culture. The creation of Pakistan, and the continued tension between India and Pakistan over the issue of Kashmir have served to foster communal feelings. The political colour to Hindu-Muslim relations was, however, given by the British who ousted the Muslim rulers and colonised India.

Although communal rifts occurred even prior to the arrival of the British, it were the British who fanned communal feelings by adopting the policy of *divide et empera*. The earlier invaders came to the land to rule and to settle; but the British motivation was quite different. They treated the country as their "colony" only to be ruled and exploited; they never

1. Rasheeduddin Khan, *Bewildered India: Identity-Pluralism Discord*, Har-Anand Publications, Delhi, 1994, p. xiv.

intended to make it their home. Always remaining "alien" they were interested in buying loyalty of the people, and dividing them so that the solidarity is broken and their hold is emboldened. It was with this intention that they introduced the system of communal representation in the management of the polity. Introduction of the process of industrialisation gave rise to competition for jobs, and encouraged people to demand share in power politics. In the process, communal considerations came to the fore.

The British were quick to exploit this situation. They succeeded in enlisting support of some of the political leaders from the two main communities—the Hindus and the Muslims—in creating communal rifts by pitting them against each other. In order to gain some political concessions, these communal leaders began lending their support to the colonial rulers. The British took advantage of the vulnerability of these leaders.

Communal feelings began to overwhelm people on both the sides during the British rule. With the arrival of the British, the Muslims lost their superior status as rulers. As deposed, they also joined the ranks of the "ruled" with the Hindus. And, they joined hands with them to oust the British, participating in a long-drawn freedom struggle. But towards the final phase of the struggle, when freedom was in sight, there arose differences between the leaders of the two communities over the sharing of power. Describing the Indian National Congress as a Hindu party, the dissident Muslim leaders formed a separate party with the tacit encouragement of the British. So as to frustrate the freedom movement, the British showed a carrot to the Muslims by proposing the partition of the country and creating a new homeland for them. It is from here that the forged unity of the freedom struggle got dissipated and seeds of distrust and antagonism between the two groups were sown. The creation of the Muslim League, and the founding of Hindu Maha Sabha were clear indications of communalisation of the freedom struggle. The British succeeded in their mission and left the country divided suffering the pangs of partition. Several lives were lost and mass migrations occurred uprooting the people of the two communities. While the Muslims who remained in Pakistan or migrated to the new country were jubilant, the Hindus in India felt frustrated over the loss of part of their motherland, and nurtured a feeling of suspicion against the Muslims. It so enraged a section of orthodox Hindus that one of the zealots even assassinated the father of the nation---Mahatma Gandhi---on 30 January 1948, regarding him as the defender of the minority community.

The creation of Pakistan gave a message to many Hindus that the Muslims as a group were not only anti-Hindu but also anti-India. Such feelings were the strongest amongst those who had to leave their land and property, in what is now Pakistan, and come to the independent India as refugees. The continued atmosphere of animosity between India and Pakistan, which gets further spoiled when wars are fought and when terrorists are sent from across the border, has never allowed mutual suspicion to die out. As a result, even the patriotic Muslims feel threatened with a sense of insecurity. Thus, whenever any steps are taken that appear to undermine the identity of their religion, the Muslims perceive them as threats and mobilise internal support to protect their interests. Special protections accorded to the minorities in the Constitution of India have served the latent, unintended function of fostering and hardening communal identities and threatening national integration. It is such developments that provoke counter-action among the so-called majority community.

Road Blocks to Secularism

The attainment of independence at the cost of partition of the country created a new crisis for the new nation. While Pakistan was carved out on the basis of religion, what remained of India---a mammoth 330 million populace---continued to be pluricultural and multi-religious. Such a country could not afford to show partiality to any particular religion. The framers of the Indian Constitution, therefore, rightly decided to keep the state religiously neutral, allowing people the freedom to practise their religion but the state remaining aloof. It is this posture that was described as "secularism".

"The Nehruvian concept of India as a secular state friendly to all religions was based on *Sarv Dharm Sadbhav* (goodwill towards all religions). Secularism was not intended to mean the negation of any religion but rather freedom of religion, and equal respect for all the religions. To usher a secular society imbibing secular temperament in its citizens in a country of multiple religions like India was a major challenge of independent India, particularly after the partition of the country in the name of religion, based on a two-nation theory. Nehru always considered it to be the special responsibility of the majority community to look to the welfare of the minorities to see that they do not get marginalized and victimized."[2]

Nehru's followers overinterpreted his concern for the minorities and reduced the notion of secularism to special safeguards and assurances to the minorities. Such a stance only helped foster and even reinvigorate communal identities and encouraged the fundamentalist leaders to obstruct the basic tenets of secularism. Oddly enough, the measures taken in the name of secularism have contributed to the weakening of secular values. See, for example, a statement by A.S. Abraham: "Minorities must not be forced in accepting any social reforms

---

2. A.D. Pant, "Nehru on Secularism and the Nature of the Secular State" in Bidyut Chakravarti (ed.), *Whither Indian Democracy*, K.P. Bagchi & Company, New Delhi, 1993, p. 167.

or common laws. Their prior consent is a must and this consent has to be won through persuasion and dialogue."[3] H.Y. Siddiqui, similarly, holds the view that "national integration is possible only when minority groups are encouraged to have their own political and cultural organizations with the sole responsibility of managing the issues on which minorities are sentimental."[4] On the other hand, some Muslim organizations began asking for proportional representation in the legislative bodies and proportional reservation of posts in government jobs, 30 per cent reservation in police and other paramilitary forces, non-application of any common civil code, elevation of Urdu to the status of second official language in some states, rewriting of the school textbooks to remove the so-called anti-minority bias, granting of statutory status to the Minority Commission which would make recommendations mandatory to the government, and total non-interference of the government in the financial affairs of their religious trusts.

Such demands by the representatives of the Muslim organisations contributed to the rise of anti-Muslim feelings among the Hindus. Their organisations justify their stand by arguing that the demands made by the Muslim organisations are indicative of their disaffection with India and the Muslims are, therefore, a threat to India's unity. They further argue that the efforts made by the government to appease the Muslims by such acts as continuous show of concern for the minorities and their rights, the establishment of Minority Commission and now giving a statutory status to it for which there was no provision in the Constitution, the exemption of minority institutions from State Regulation, etc., would only strengthen

3. "Concept of Minoritism: An agenda for Theocracy" in *The Times of India*, 10 December 1990.
4. Saral Jhingran, *Secularism in India: A Reappraisal*, Har-Anand Publications, New Delhi, 1995, p. 211.

their sense of separate communal identity, obstructing their participation in the national mainstream. That the word "minority" can create problems was realised even at the time when the constitution of free India was on the anvil. Thus, speaking during the Constituent Assembly debate on denominational rights, Tajmal Hussain said: "I want to tell the House that there is no minority in this country. I do not consider myself a minority. In a secular state there is no such thing as minority. I wish those who consider themselves as the majority community would forget that there is any minority today in the country."[5]

Equally assertive of the opposite point of view, favouring *Hindutva* are the statements of the RSS leader, M.S. Golwalkar and journalist Girilal Jain. Golwalkar expressed his dislike for the word "minority". In his own peculiar style, he said: "There are some people who claim that they have achieved unity of Hindus, Muslims, Christians and all others on the political and economic plain. But why limit this oneness there only? Why not make it wider and more comprehensive, so as to fuse them all in a Hindu way of life, in our *dharma* and take them back as lost brothers? We stand not only for political and economic unity but also for cultural and religious unity. Undoubtedly, this is a broader outlook."[6] Girilal Jain[7] also identified India with Hinduism and Hindu culture. He also rejected the thesis of synthetic Indian culture developed during the Mughal period. He asserted: "Hindus should have declared India as a *Hindu Rashtra* in 1947 itself as Pakistan was declared an Islamic state."[8]

5. Ibid., p. 219.

6. *Bunch of Thoughts,* p.133 as quoted in Moin Shakir's, *Politics of Minorities*, Ajanta Publications, New Delhi, 1980, p. 11.

7. Who was editor of *The Times of India.*

8. Saral Jhingran, op. cit., p. 222.

There are scholars who believe that Hindus never existed in the sense of a unified Hindu community. They argue that the Hindus are not only divided into a large number of castes, but they also worship different types of gods, and there is nothing like a "common church". Hinduism, in fact, is an intensely pluralistic conception. Even the BJP leadership claims that its insistence on *Hindutva* as the basis of Indian nationalism was not anti-secular at all because they contend that the word 'Hindu' is merely the term for every inhabitant of India. Thus, they would argue that the Christians, Muslims and Parsees living in India are merely Hindu Christians, Hindu Parsees and Hindu Muslims respectively. According to BJP, the term 'Hindu' denotes geographical nationalism and has nothing to do with Hindu religion.[9]

Despite these pronouncements, the BJP tried to unite the caste Hindus and used several tactics to mobilise them for political purposes. They even constantly instigated the Hindus for aggressive self-assertion: *Garv Se Kaho Ki Ham Hindu Hain* (say with pride that we are Hindus). The party also projected negative stereotypes of the Muslims.

In contrast, the Congress generally remained aloof when Hindu and Muslim extremists tried to polarise the Indian society along religious lines. Maintaining its so-called secular stance it did voice its criticism against the Hindu organisations and extended favours to the minorities. But these were seen as attempts to create "vote banks". In course of time, when actions of the minorities began to directly hurt the majority community, Congress changed its strategy so as not to lose its support base among the Hindus. It became ambivalent when secessionist groups in Punjab, Kashmir and Assam attacked the Hindus. Indira Gandhi went out of her way to appease the

9. H.K. Parnajapee, "Secularism: The Real or Pseudo", *Mainstream*, Vol. XXIX, No.30, May 1991.

Hindu voters by decrying the secessionist acts. She even allowed herself to be equated with "Durga"—a Hindu goddess. Meenakshipuram conversions that attracted India-wide protests by the Hindus compelled her to take the Hindu side and even declare that Hinduism is in danger.

The 1980s thus created a situation where the "Hindu card" was played both by the BJP and the Congress. This necessitated the BJP and its allies to rethink their strategy to prevent Congress from penetrating into its support base. In the process, communalism got more politicised.

The Politics of the 1980s

The emergence of communal politics in the 1980s can be broadly attributed to an overall shift in the mobilisation strategy of the Congress party and the consequent reaction to it by the BJP. The Ayodhya dispute, which began purely as a legal battle over a piece of land between two religious communities, became a political issue only when political parties started taking interest in it and using the dispute to their political advantage.

The Congress projected itself as a party promoting communal peace and as committed to solve the dispute by respecting the religious sentiments of both Hindus and Muslims. On the other hand, the BJP projected itself as a party protecting the interest of the Hindus. This created a sense of insecurity and suspicion in the minds of Muslims. The Muslim organisations put forth their claim for justice and expected the ruling party to take its side in refuting the claims of the Hindu party by supporting the Muslim claim over the disputed structure. The fact of the matter was that all the parties—be it the Congress, Janata Dal or BJP—were guided by electoral considerations and, thus, were keen to keep the issue alive. The sustained mobilisation efforts by all the parties prior to the general elections of 1989 show that this was a political issue and all of them were trying to build their own vote banks. And this issue indeed paid off politically to them. The BJP and Janata Dal increased their polling support. The Congress party also tried to play the Hindu card by allowing the *shilanyas* on the disputed site. However, it could not get the support of the entire Hindu community that suspected its real intentions, whereas the BJP and Janata Dal were able to get support of Hindus and Muslims respectively. In the 10th general elections (1991) also, this issue became the major plank in the election campaign. But, the BJP was the main gainer because it was firm and consistent in its stand for the construction of Ram Temple. This put BJP at the centre stage of Indian politics, where it successfully associated other issues like pseudo-secularism, minoritism, nationalism and *Hindutva* in a very subtle manner and got the support of wide spectrum of Hindu society virtually forcing every party to redefine the concept of secularism as the main agenda of Indian politics.

According to the BJP, the Ayodhya dispute was a crusade against the pseudo-secular policy of the Congress. It wanted to reopen a national debate on secularism. In its manifesto for 9th and 10th general elections, the BJP stated that it believed in positive secularism which, according to the makers of Indian Constitution, meant *Sarv Dharm Sambhav* (equal respect for all religions) and which did not connote the concept of an irreligious or non-religious state. "It certainly does not mean the rejection of our cultural heritage, the very foundation of this great nation. The BJP stood for justice for all, and appeasement for none."[10] BJP's stand on the question of Ram Mandir, Article 370 and the Uniform Civil Code, created fear-psychosis among the Muslims who thought that the BJP was trying to reduce them to the status of "second-class citizens".

10. *BJP Manifesto for 9th General Election*, p. 7.

BJP's argument in defence of its stand on the Uniform Civil Code was that Article 44 of the Constitution, enjoining the state to secure a Uniform Civil Code for all its citizens was nothing new. It argued that even Dr. Ambedkar, Dr. Rajendra Prasad, Jawaharlal Nehru, Maulana Azad and Sardar Patel had supported the idea. If BJP's demand for a Uniform Civil Code makes it "communal", then by the same token, these leaders will also have to be characterised as "communal". BJP emphasised the point that it should not be marked out to be communal or anti-Muslim because it was simply reiterating what was written in the Indian Constitution. Regarding Article 25 of the Constitution, which gives the state the power to legislate for the social welfare and reforms of Hindu religious institutions only while making no such provisions for any other religion, BJP's stand was that "it was an insult to the Hindu religious institutions". It, therefore, wanted it to be amended. It did not regard this demand for amendment a communal or anti-Muslim demand. Again, in regard to Article 30, BJP holds the view that either let every community administer its own educational institutions without state intervention or remove the special exemption given to the minorities in this regard.[11]

Muslim fundamentalists have always regarded BJP as a communal party complaining that it talks only about Hindu interests. What is important to note is that there are other parties also which are equally responsible for playing the communal card. V.P. Singh and Mulayam Singh Yadav are also examples of playing the minority game. In order to saddle into power, V.P. Singh of Janata Dal refused to share the public platform with BJP leaders in 1989 elections despite having electoral seat adjustments with BJP. On the other hand, he openly moved in the company of Shahi Imam of Jama Masjid

11. M.N. Buch, "Who is Secular?" *The Hindustan Times*, 17 May 1996.

who made public announcements for the support of V.P. Singh and his Janata Dal. Similarly, in order to get Muslim votes, Mulayam Singh Yadav of Samajvadi (Socialist) Party made very provocative and objectionable speeches against the Hindus to counter the proposed *kar seva* in 1990 by VHP at Ayodhya, while holding *sadbhavana* (goodwill) rallies. Even the left parties, which claim to be truly secular, had alliances with the Indian Union Muslim League in Kerala. Similarly, when UDF government of Kerala declared that Muslim majority schools would have their weekly holiday on Fridays instead of Sundays, and that all schools would have a mid-afternoon break so that Muslim students may say their *Namaz*, people interpreted it as an encouragement to religious orthodoxy, and hurting the feelings of the non-Muslims. The left parties of Kerala did not oppose such communal measures, ostensibly for fear of losing the Muslim vote.

Although the Indian Constitution described the country as a secular state, in practice, all political parties indulge in the vote bank politics. In selecting candidates for a given constituency, the parties take into account the numerical preponderance of a caste or religious community and generally give tickets to those who belong to the dominant group in the constituency in question. Even the Congress party, which fought for the independence of the country under the guidance of Gandhi and Nehru, follows this strategy.

The Ayodhya dispute, particularly the dismantling of the mosque, was not confined to a single party. Allegations are that even the Congress government covertly supported this because it could not afford to ignore the concerns of the majority community.

The disputed mosque was kept under lock and key until the district court ordered its opening and the Congress government went along with it so as to appease the Hindus who were earlier unhappy about the government stand on the Shah Bano case.

The Congress government played a game of dual appeasement---first appeasing conservative Muslims in the Shah Bano case, and then the VHP by opening the gates of the disputed shrine for Hindus to perform worship of the idol of Lord Ram there. It was the Congress government of Rajiv Gandhi, which allowed the laying of foundation stone for the temple in 1989. Once such steps had been taken to open the gates and allow the worship, it literally opened the doors for further conflict between the two communities. Reacting to the Congress party's role, *The Times of India*, in its editorial, said: "The alienation of Muslims will undoubtedly mark as the most grievous lapse on the part of Rajiv Gandhi government. In retrospect, the laying of the foundation stone of the Ram Temple in Ayodhya on 9 November 1989 can be seen to be a dangerous turning point in the history of independent India. The seeds of disintegration of the secular vision of the country were sown on that day. History cannot easily pardon the Congress for the direct and indirect contribution to the spectacular growth of Hindu chauvinist forces today and for the tightening hold of the fundamentalist on the Muslim community."[12]

Commenting on the communal and caste conflicts in India, Paul R. Brass in his book, *The Politics of India since Independence*, writes:

> It is necessary to seek the sources of broader anti-Muslim hostility not only among Hindu communal ideologies and organisations, but in the secular ideology which, since Independence, has exalted the state and its unity as the highest political value and has in the process placed the state at the center of the communal question, assigning it the role of preventing disintegrative communal conflict and protecting "minorities". Nehru himself and Mrs. Gandhi more so appealed to Muslims for support by implying

12. *The Times of India*, 28 November 1989.

that their own safety against Hindu communalists could be ensured only by remaining loyal to the Congress. Toward the end of her life, Mrs. Gandhi's opportunism on this matter was further revealed by the shift of the Congress under her leadership toward appeals to Hindu sentiment, carried further by her son, Rajiv, in the 1984 and 1989 elections.[13]

Harold Gould—an anthropologist and a keen observer of Uttar Pradesh politics for several years, also shares this view. In his brilliant analysis of the Babri Masjid episode he has devoted a full section on "Congress' role in the promotion of anti-secular processes". He writes:

> ...even in Nehru's day, there had been much ambivalence in the Congress party itself on the issue of what secularism should mean, especially with regard to what policies should be adopted toward the country's 'mega-minority', the Muslims. In certain respects, this ambivalence helped pave the way for the Babri Masjid's destruction in 1992, and certainly influenced its political aftermath, as indeed it had paved the way for the *murtis* incident in 1949.[14]

Gould goes on to say that the decade of the 1980s marked a significant change in Indian polity. He writes:

> The period between 1986 and 1992 changed everything. For the first time since independence, a secular government compromised its unambiguous affirmation of secular (i.e., ethno-accommodative) principles and colluded with the proponents of the ethnoreligious state...The Sangh Parivar's claim that its advocacy of the ethnoreligious state represented the restoration of

13. Paul R. Brass, *The Politics of India since Independence*, Cambridge University Press, Second Edition, 1997, pp.264-65.

14. Harold Gould, "The Babri Masjid and the secular contract" in *Tradition, Pluralism, and Identity* (edited by Veena Das et al.), Sage Publications, New Delhi, 1999. p.394.

> an original Hindu culture and statecraft is a classic manifestation of the *ex post facto* invention (or reworking) of a tradition to fit contemporary political stratagems.....By acceding to the unlocking of the Babri Masjid and then remaining passive when the mosque was torn down by the Vishwa Hindu Parishad, Congress helped to facilitate this reworking of tradition to accommodate the Sangh Parivar's political agenda, and by doing so cut the moral ground out from under itself...[15]

Final Comment

Communalism is affecting the entire Indian political process of the day. Electoral system has been largely distorted owing to the communalisation of the secular polity. In view of the peculiarities of vote bank politics, almost all the political parties unhesitatingly exploit the caste, communal, regional and linguistic factors in their quest for political power

In post-independent India several communal riots on petty issues occurred but they were generally localised. But, the electoral politics of the country brought these rifts into limelight and all parties exploited this aspect to gain political mileage. Interestingly enough, communalism got greater encouragement by those parties, which professed secularism. In the name of secularism, they showed overconcern to the cause of minority communities to the virtual neglect of the majority community. Yogesh Atal, in his article titled "The Fetish of Secularism" published in *The Hindustan Times* (29 April 1999) aptly commented on this development:

> Parties are vying with each other to demonstrate their secular character by taking the side of the minority groups...It is ironical that being partial to such groups is defined as being secular, and taking the cause of the majority group is termed communal.

15. Ibid., pp.397-98.

He is of the view that "to think that only protecting the interest of the minority groups is secularism is to change the definition of the very concept". It is the attitude adopted by the so-called secular parties that the parties characterised as "communal" have begun strongly reacting to demonstrate the falsity of their claims.

The paradox of Indian political system is that while the state has been declared as secular, the society is getting increasingly communalised. Such a situation throws innumerable challenges to the polity and the society at large. Politics is a game of numbers for which each political party needs certain vote banks. This has forced every party to use every available opportunity to get votes using communal, linguistic, caste or regional issues. There is no political party, including the Congress or left parties, which has not embraced professedly communal overtones in electoral adjustments and alliances as well as in the formation of coalition governments. There is no political party in the country that has not mobilized communal and caste organisations or has resisted the lure of communal arithmetic while planning the electoral strategy. It can be argued that if BJP's appeal to Hindus for electoral support is communal, then an appeal to Muslims alone as a religious group to vote in a particular manner is equally communal. In such a communally charged atmosphere, there is a need for the inculcation of genuine secular values and ethos in almost all the facets of Indian life, and not just in the affairs of the state.

The social fabric of Indian society is under severe strain. Hindus and Muslims are resorting to various types of revivalism which all go to foster communalism. The very edifice of India's glorious composite culture, that has evolved over centuries of accommodation and assimilation is being torn apart by narrow concerns and invocation of primordial loyalties.

The responsibility of the state is very important in preserving the secular ethos of the country. The state should maintain distance from all religions and work hard to promote inter-religious amity and cordiality. Without separating religion from polity, the church from the state, it is inherently impossible to ensure a functioning democracy.

Secularism should neither be reduced either to pseudo-secularism or to what BJP calls "positive secularism", nor should it be subjected to opportunism and subtle form of communalism as is practised by the Congress. In fact, both Nehru's vision of secularism and BJP's concept of positive secularism have their inherent loopholes that need to be corrected.

A pluralistic society, that India of today is, cannot survive in an atmosphere of communal disharmony. Understood as an ideology of peaceful co-existence and mutual respect for each other's religion and values, secularism paves the way for creating unity and diversity. It is the cultural symbiosis that makes the diversity creative. We must acknowledge the fact that the forces of modernisation have not been able to homogenise the world into a single monolith of world culture. Societies have modernised, but have remained heterogeneous. It should also be emphasised that any society---be it homogeneous or heterogeneous---is, to quote MacIver and Page, "cooperation crossed by conflict". Conflicts arise in any living society and cultural and social processes come into operation to resolve them and bring society to its normalcy that is characterised by cooperation. To be sure, resolution of one conflict is not a guarantee that new conflicts would not arise in the future. It is the capacity of the society to anticipate such conflicts and take timely action to prevent them that determines its continuity. As such, there are no panaceas for a conflict-free society. Conflicts are a fact of life and require society's readiness to resolve them. India's commitment to secularism continues to be the guiding principle for the promotion of cooperation and prevention of conflict. Communalistic trends have given rise to a sub-culture of conflict. Given the plurality of the Indian society, occasional rise of primordial loyalties can easily be anticipated; what will be needed is to ensure that such loyalties do not lead to group insularity. Communal identities may not be erased, and yet there can be effective interpenetration of cultural traits to ensure furtherance of a composite culture.

The path to a genuine and clean secularity is indeed a long and arduous one entailing many pragmatic adjustments on the way. But these pragmatic adjustments should never become intellectual compromises. If they do so, the concept of secularism will be enfeebled, the goal of national unity will be forgotten, and we will be lost as a nation broken down into isolated islands of a non-communicative archipelago.

Bibliography

Books

Aggarwal J.C. and N.K. Chowdhry, *Ram Janam Bhoomi Through the Ages: Babri Masjid Controversy* (Delhi: S. Chand & Company Ltd., 1991).

--- (eds.), *Elections in India (From 1952 to By-Elections 1991): Analysis and Overview* (Delhi: Shipra Publications, 1992).

Ahuja, Gurdas M., *BJP and the Indian Politics: Policies and Programmes of the BJP* (Delhi: Suruchi Prakashan, 1994).

Ahuja, M.L. and Sharda Paul (eds.), *General Elections in India 1989-91* (New Delhi: Associated Publishing House, 1992).

Anderson, Walter K. and Sridhar D. Damle (eds.), *The Brotherhood in Saffron: The Rashtriya Swayamsevak Sangh and Hindu Revivalism* (London: Western Press, 1987).

Arslan, Mehdi and Janaki Rajan (eds.), *Communalism in India: Challenge and Response* (New Delhi: Manohar Publications, 1994).

Atal, Yogesh, *Dynamics of Nation Building: Communities in Crisis Situation, Vol. II* (Bangkok: Rushsop, 1988).

—, *Local Communities and National Politics* (Delhi: National Publishing House, 1971).

Banu, Zenab, *Politics of Communalism: A Politico-Historical Analysis of*

Communal Riots in Post-Independence India with Reference to Gujarat and Rajasthan Riots (Bombay: Popular Publications, 1989).

Basu, Tapan, Pradip Datta, Sumit Sarkar, Tanika Sarkar, *Khaki Shorts Saffron Flags: A Critique of the Hindu Rights* (New Delhi: Orient Longman, 1993).

Baxter, Craig, *The Jana Sangh: A Biography of an Indian Political Party* (Philadelphia, USA: University of Pennsylvania Press, 1969).

Bhambhri, C.P., *Elections 1991: An Analysis* (Delhi: B.R. Publishing Company, 1991).

—, *India's Struggle for Independence 1857-1947* (New Delhi: Vikas Publications, 1988).

—, *Indian Politics Since Independence* (Delhi: Shipra Publications, 1994).

Bipan Chandra, *Communalism in Modern India* (New Delhi: Vikas Publications, 1987).

—, *India's Struggle for Independence: 1857-1947* (New Delhi: Vikas Publishing House, 1988).

—, *Essays on Contemporary India* (New Delhi: Har Anand Publications, 1993).

Brass, Paul R., *Caste, Faction and Party in Indian Politics, Vol. II, Election Studies* (Delhi: Chanakya Publications, 1985).

—, *The Cambridge History of India: Politics of India Since Independence* (Hyderabad: Cambridge University Press, 1990).

Butler, David, Ashok Lahiri and Pronnoy Roy, *India Decides: Elections 1952-1991* (New Delhi: Living Media India Ltd., 1991).

Census of India, 1981, Paper 1 Religion.

Census of India, Series No.1, Paper 1 of 1991 Religion.

Chakrabarty, Bidyut (ed.), *Secularism and Indian Polity* (New Delhi: Segment Book Distributors, 1990).

—, *Whither Indian Democracy* (New Delhi: K.P. Bagchi & Company, 1993).

Das, Arvind N., *India Invented: A Nation in the Making* (New Delhi: Manohar Publications, 1992).

Das, Veena, Dipankar Gupta and Patricia Oberoi (eds), *Tradition, Pluralism and Identity* (New Delhi: Sage Publications, 1999).

Deoki Nandan, *Sri Rama Janma Bhumi: Historical and Legal Perspective* (New Delhi: VHP Publication (n.d.)).

Dhar, Pannalal, *India and Her Domestic Problems: Religion, State and Secularism* (Calcutta: Punthi Pustak, 1993).

Dixit, Prabha, *Communalism: A Struggle for Power* (New Delhi: Orient Longman, 1974).

Dutt, R.C. (ed.), *People and Politics: The Indian Experience* (New Delhi: Lancer Publishers, 1992).

Engineer, Asghar Ali, *Communalism and Communal Violence in India: An Analytical Approach to Hindu Muslim Conflict* (Delhi: Ajanta Publications, 1989).

—, *Babri Masjid-Ram Janam Bhoomi Controversy* (New Delhi: Ajanta Publications, 1990).

—, *Lifting the Veil: Communal Violence and Communal Harmony in Contemporary India* (Hyderabad: Sangam Books India Ltd., 1995).

— (ed.), *Communal Riots in Post-Independence India* (Bombay: Sangam Books, 1984).

—, *The Role of Minorities in Freedom Struggle* (Delhi: Ajanta Publications, 1986).

—, (ed.), *The Shah Bano Controversy* (Hyderabad: Orient Longman, 1987).

— (ed.), *The Politics of Confrontation: The Babri Masjid Ramjanambhoomi Controversy Ruins & Riots* (Delhi: Ajanta Publications, 1992).

— and Moin Shakir (eds.), *Communalism in India* (Delhi: Ajanta Publications, 1985).

— and Pradeep Nayak (ed.), *Communalisation of Politics and 10th Lok Sabha Elections* (New Delhi: Ajanta Publications, 1993).

Freitag, Sandria, *Collective Action and Community: Public Arenas and the Emergence of Communalism in North India* (Delhi: Oxford University Press, 1990).

Gahrana, Kanan, *Right to Freedom of Religion: A Study in Indian Secularism* (New Delhi: ICSSR Publications, 1992).

Gehlot, N.S. (ed.), *Politics of Communalism and Secularism: Keeping Indians Divided* (New Delhi: Deep and Deep Publications, 1993).

Ghosh, Partha S., *BJP and the Evolution of Hindu Nationalism*, (New Delhi, Manohar, 1999).

Ghosh, S.K., *Muslim Politics in India* (New Delhi: Ashish Publications, 1987).

Gopal, Sarvepalli (ed.), *Anatomy of Confrontation: The Babri Masjid Ram Janambhoomi Issue* (New Delhi: Penguin Books India Ltd., 1991).

Gore, M.S. (ed.), *Secularism in India* (Allahabad: Vindhya Prakashan Pvt Ltd. Company, 1991).

Graham, Bruce D., *Hindu Nationalism and Indian Politics: The Origins and Development of the Bharatiya Jana Sangh* (New York: Cambridge University Press, 1991).

Gupta, A.L. (ed.), *Confrontational Politics in India* (New Delhi: Commonwealth Publishers, 1984).

Gupta, Raghuraj, *Hindu-Muslim Relations* (Lucknow: Ethnographic and Folk Cultural Society, 1976).

Haqqi, S.A.H., *Secularism under Siege: The Ayodhya Tragedy in Retrospect and Prospect* (Aligarh: U.P. Rohit Committee, 1993).

Hasan, Mushirul, (ed.), *Communal and Pan Islamic Trends in Colonial India* (New Delhi: Manohar, 1985).

Hasan, Zoya, *State, Political Processes and Identity, Reflections of Modern India*, (New Delhi: Sage Publications, 1989).

—, *Dominance and Mobilisation, Rural Politics in Western UP, 1930-1980* (New Delhi: Sage Publications, 1989).

Hunter, W.W., *The Indian Musalmaans* (Lahore: Premier Book House, 1968).

Jhingran, Saral, *Secularism in India: A Reappraisal* (New Delhi: Har Anand Publications, 1995).

Kabir, Humayun, *Minorities in a Democracy* (Calcutta: K.L. Mukhopadhyay, 1968).

Kesavani, Mukul, *Communal Violence and Its Impact on the Politics of North India 1937-1939*, Occasional Paper (New Delhi: Nehru Memorial Museum & Library, Teen Murti House).

Khan, M. Rafiq, *Forms of Communalism, National Integration: Its Meaning and Relevance* (Varanasi: Navchetna Prakashan, 1970).

Khan, Rasheeduddin, *Bewildered India: Identity, Pluralism, Discard* (Delhi: Har Anand Publications, 1994).

Khan, Syed Ahmed, *An Account of Loyal Mohammedans of India* (Meerut, 1860).

Kolnraad, Elst, *Ayodhya and After: Issues before Hindu Society* (New Delhi: Voice of India, 1990).

—, *Ram Janambhoomi Vs Babri Masjid: A Case Study in Hindu- Muslim Conflict* (New Delhi: Voice of India, 1990).

Kothari, Rajni, *State Against Democracy: In Search of Humane Governance* (Delhi: Asia Publications, 1988).

Kumar, Akhilesh, *Communal Riots in India: Study of Social and Economic Aspects* (New Delhi: Commonwealth Publishers, 1991).

Kumar, Pramod (ed.), *Towards Understanding Communalism* (Chandigarh: Centre of Research in Rural and Industrial Development, 1992).

—, *Polluting Sacred Faith: A Study of Communalism and Violence in India* (Delhi: Ajanta Publications, 1992).

Malik, Yogendra K. and V.B. Singh (eds.), *Hindu Nationalists in India: The Rise of the BJP* (Westview Press, U.S.A., 1994).

Malkani, K.R., *The Politics of Ayodhya and Hindu-Muslim Relations* (New Delhi: Har Anand Publications, 1993).

Mehra, V.R., *Ideology, Modernisation and Politics in India* (New Delhi: Manohar Publications, 1983).

Mitra, Subrota (ed.), *Electoral Politics in India: A Changing Landscape* (New Delhi: Segment Books, 1992).

Morris-Jones, W.H., *The Government and Politics in India* (London: Hutchinson, 1971).

Naidu, Ratna, *Communal Edges to Plural Societies: India and Malaysia* (New Delhi: Vikas Publishing House, 1980).

Nandy, Ashis, Shikha Trivedi, Shail Mayaram, Achyut Yagnik, *Creating a Nationality* (Delhi: Oxford University Press, 1995).

Nayak, Pradeep, *The Politics of Ayodhya Dispute: Rise of Communalism and Future Voting Behaviour* (New Delhi: Commonwealth Publications, 1993).

Nizami, Z.A., *Hakim Ajmal Khan* (New Delhi: Publications Division, Ministry of Information & Broadcasting, 1988).

Padmashah, *Indian National Congress and the Muslims 1928-1947* (New Delhi: Rajash Publications).

Pandey, Deepak, *The Role of Muslim League in National Politics* (Delhi: Tiwari Publications: 1991).

Pandey, G., *The Ascendancy of Congress in U.P., 1926-34: A Study in Imperfect Mobilisation* (New Delhi: Oxford University Press, 1978).

—, *Construction of Communalism in Colonial North India* (New Delhi: Oxford University Press, 1990).

—, *Hindus and Others: The Question of Identity in India* (New Delhi: Viking Publications, 1993).

Pannikar, K.N. (ed.), *Communalism in India: History, Politics and Culture* (New Delhi: Manohar Publications, 1991).

Prasad, Rajendra, *India Divided* (Bombay: Hind Kitabs, 1946).

Puri, Geeta, *Bharatiya Jana Sangh: Organisation and Ideology* (New Delhi: Sterling Publishers, 1980).

Qasimi, Mawana Asrarul Haque, *The Community in Retrospect* (Delhi, n.d.).

Rajgopal, P.R., *Communal Violence in India* (New Delhi: Uppal Publishers, 1987).

Ramji Lal, *Communal Problem in India: A Symposium* (Karnal: Dyal Singh College Publications, 1988).

Rana, M.S. (ed), *Manifestoes of National Parties: Indian Elections, 1991* (Roorkee: Uma Rani Publications, 1993).

Rao, K. Raghavendra, *Religion, Society and State* (New Delhi: ICSSR Publications, 1992).

Robinson, Francis, *Separatism among Indian Muslims* (Delhi: Vikas Publishing House, 1975).

Saksena, N.S., *Communal Riots in India*, (Noida: Trishul Publications, 1990).

Shakir, Moin, *Politics of Minorities* (New Delhi: Ajanta Publications, 1980).

--- (ed.), *Religion, State and Politics in India* (Delhi: Ajanta Publications, 1989).

Sharma, R.S., *Communal History and Ram's Ayodhya* (New Delhi: People's Publishing House, 1990).

Shourie, Arun, *A Secular Agenda* (Delhi: ASA Publication, 1993).

—, *Indian Controversies: Essays on Religion in Politics* (Delhi: ASA Publications, 1993).

Singh, V.B. and Shankar Bose (eds.), *State Elections in India: Data Handbook on Vidhan Sabha Elections 1952-85* (New Delhi: Sage Publications, 1987).

Singh, V.V., *Communal Violence* (Jaipur: Rawat Publications,1993).

South Asia (Journal of South Asian Studies - Special Issue, Vol. XVII (Australia: South Asian Studies Association, 1994).

Thursby, G.R., *Hindu Muslim Relations in British India: A Study of Controversy, Conflict, and Communal Movements in Northern India, 1923-1928* (Leiden, Netherlands: E.J. Brill, 1975).

Vajpayee, Atal Bihari, *India at the Crossroads* (New Delhi: A BJP Publication, 1980).

Vishwa Hindu Parishad, *The Saga of Ayodhya* (Jagrama Prakashan Trust, Bangalore, 1990).

Wadhwa, Kamlesh Kumar, *Minority Safeguards in India* (Thomson Press Ltd., Publication Division, 1975).

Zakaria, Rafiq, *The Widening Divide, An Insight Into Hindu-Muslim Relations* (New Delhi: Penguin Books, 1991).

Articles

Agha, Zafar, "BJP: Brinkmanship Backfires", *India Today*, 15 February 1992.

Ahmad, Imtiaz, "Political Economy of Communalism in

Contemporary India", *Economic and Political Weekly*, 2-9 June 1984.

Aiyar, Shahnaz Anklesaria, "BJP: Aiming High", *India Today*, 15 May 1991.

—, "BJP: Counting the Gains", *India Today*, 29 February 1992.

Atal, Yogesh, "Ideological Proximities, Political Distances", *Young India*, April 24-May 1, 1999.

Bamzai, Kaveree, "Ekta Yatra: An Odyssey of Futility", *India Today*, 15 February 1992.

Bano Zenab, "A Political Scientist's View of Communalism", in *Communalism in India*, (eds. Asghar Ali Engineer and Moin Shakir) Ajanta Publication, Delhi, 1985.

Baweja, Narinder, "Ekta Yatra: Smooth Ride", *India Today*, 31 January 1992.

Bhambhri, C.P., "Practice of Secularism", *Muslim India*, April 1995.

Bidwai, Praful, "BJP's Ekta Yatra: A Recipe for Disunity", *The Times of India* (New Delhi), 13 December 1991.

Bipan Chandra, "BJP, RSS and Nationalism", *Link*, 13 October 1991.

—, "Communalism in Retrospect", *Mainstream*, 18 August 1984.

Buch, M.N., "Who is Secular?", *The Hindustan Times*, 17 May 1996.

Chadha, Kumkum, "Will the BJP be Banned ?", *The Hindustan Times* (New Delhi), 20 December 1992.

Chakraborty, Bidyut, "Communalism in Indian Politics", *The Journal of Asian Studies*, April 1986.

Chawla, Prabha and Pankaj Pachauri, "BJP on the Warpath", *India Today*, 31 October 1990.

Dasgupta, Swapan, "BJP: A Party in the Making", *Seminar*, May 1994.

Engineer, Asghar Ali, "Communalism as Poll Weapon", *Indian Express* (New Delhi), 5 December 1989.

—, "Communalism: Its Facets and Roots", *Mainstream*, 28 June 1986.

—, "On Secularism and Pseudo-Secularism", *Mainstream*, 22 June 1991.

Gandhi, Krishna, "Anatomy of Muradabad Riots", *Economic and Political Weekly*, 6 September 1980.

Ganguli, Amulya, "Ayodhya Aftermath: Lessons from BJP's Retreat", *The Times of India* (New Delhi), 19 April 1993.

---, "Ayodhya to Idgah: Emotions as Political Weapon", *The Times of India* (New Delhi), 22 August 1994.

---, "Waves in Elections: The Absence of Ram Lehar", *The Times of India* (New Delhi), 15 November 1993).

Ghimire, Yubaraj, "BJP: Bracing for the Bigger Battles", *India Today*, 30 April 1995.

Gopal, Krishna, "Communal Issues Revisited", *The Times of India*, 10 October 1974.

Gould, Harold, "The Babri Masjid and the Secular Contract" in *Tradition, Pluralism and Identity* (eds. Veena Das et al.) Sage Publications, New Delhi, 1999.

Graf, Violet, "The Muslim Vote" in *Electoral Politics in India: A Changing Landscape* (ed. Subrota Mitra), New Delhi, Segment Books, 1992.

Gupta, Smita and Vidya Subrahmaniam, "Uttar Pradesh: A State Divided" in *Politics of Confrontation: The Babri Masjid-Ramjanmabhoomi Controversy, Ruins and Riots* (ed. by Asghar Engineer) New Delhi, Ajanta Publications, 1992.

Hafiz, M.A., "BJP Mood Upbeat Again in U.P.", *The Hindustan Times* (New Delhi), 4 June 1995.

Hasan, Zoya Khaliq, "Communalism and Communal Violence in India" *Social Scientist*, February 1982.

Hasan, Zoya, "Communalism and Communal Violence in India", in *Communal Riots in Post-Independent India*, (ed. Asghar Ali Engineer) Bombay, Sangam Books, 1984.

Khan, Rasheeduddin, "Communalism: Dimensions and Challenge", *Lest View*, December 1996.

Limaye, Madhu, "A Travesty of Hindu Dharma", *The Hindustan Times* (New Delhi) 17 January 1993.

Malik, Yogendra K. and V.B. Singh, "BJP: An Alternative to the Congress", *Asian Survey*, April 1992.

Malkani, K.R., "Significance of Ayodhya: Working out the Indic Thesis, Anti Thesis and Synthesis", *Indian Express* (Kochin), 3 August 1992.

Mehta, Vinod, "Thank You and Good Bye", *Sunday*, 20 November 1989.

Narain, Iqbal, "Future of Democracy in India: Some Reflections in the Context of Tenth Lok Sabha Poll Verdict", *The Indian Journal of Social Science*, April-June 1992.

Noorani, A.G., "BJP: Child of RSS and Heir to Hindu Mahasabha, *Mainstream*, 27 July 1991.

---, "BJP's Talking Point: Its Concept of Nationalism and Secularism", *Frontline*, 25 May-7 June 1991.

---, "Legal Aspects of the Issue" in *Anatomy of Confrontation: The Babri Masjid and Ramjanambhoomi* (ed. S. Gopal), New Delhi, Penguin Books, 1991.

Panikkar, K.N., "A Historical Overview" in *Anatomy of Confrontation: The Babri Masjid and Ramjanambhoomi Issues* (ed. S. Gopal). New Delhi, Penguin Books, 1991.

Panikkar, Lalita, "A Legal History of Temple-Mosque Dispute", *The Times of India*, 8 December 1990.

Pant, A.D., "Nehru on Secularism and the Nature of Secular State" in *Whither Indian Democracy*? (ed. Bidyut Chakravarti), New Delhi, K.P. Bagchi & Co., 1993.

Paranjapee, H.K., "Secularism: The Real or Pseudo", *Mainstream*, Vol. XXIX, No.30, May 1991.

"Politics of Communal Secularism", *Indian Express* (New Delhi), 20 September 1989.

Pramod Kumar and Bhupender Yadav, "Communalism and National Integration, I&II", *Mainstream*, 9 and 16 February 1985.

Puri, Balraj, "Communalism and Regionalism", *Economic and Political Weekly*, 11 July 1987.

—, "Lessons of Ayodhya", *The Hindustan Times* (New Delhi), 31 December 1992.

Ramaswamy, Cho. S., "Ayodhya: A Warning", *The Hindustan Times* (New Delhi), 20 December 1992.

Saberwal, Satish, and Mushirul Hasan, "Moradabad Riots 1980: Causes and Meanings" in *Communal Riots in Post-Independent India*, (ed. Asghar Ali Engineer) Bombay, Sangam Books, 1984.

Shah, A.B., "The Facts of Communalism", *The Secularist*, No.8, December 1970.

Singh, Randhir, "Communalism in Contemporary India: Some Theoretical Considerations", *Mainstream*, 14 November 1992.

---, "Theorising Communalism", *Economic and Political Weekly*, July 1988.

Singh, Randhir, "Communalism and the Structural Against Communalism: A Marxist View", in Communalism in India: History, Politics and Culture (ed. K.N. Panikar) New Delhi, Manohar Publications, 1991.

Subramaniam, K., "Communalism and Nation-State Building" in *Towards Understanding Communalism* (Promad Kumar) Centre of Research in Rural and Industrial Development, Chandigarh, 1992.

Sunil Kumar, "The Communal Divide in the Post-Independence India: The Role of the BJP in the 1980s", *Teaching Politics*, 1992.

Thapar, Romila, "Imagined Religious Communities? Ancient History and the Modern Search for a Hindu Identity", *Modern Asian Studies*, 1989.

---, "Politics of Religious Community", *Seminar*, Vol.365, January 1992.

Van der Veer, Peter,"God Must be Liberated: A Hindu Liberation Movement in Ayodhya," *Modern Asian Studies*, Vol. 21, No.2, 1987.

Index